THE SCOOP
from
"BIRD POOP"

35 YEARS OF WILD BIRD RESCUES

Bebe McCasland

Illustrations by
Don Collins

bright sky press
HOUSTON, TEXAS

bright sky press
HOUSTON, TEXAS

2365 Rice Blvd., Suite 202 Houston, Texas 77005

Copyright © 2009 Bebe McCasland; Illustrations Copyright © 2009 Don Collins

ISBN 978-1-933979-52-6

10 9 8 7 6 5 4 3 2 1

Library of Congress information on file with publisher.

Book and cover design by Tutu Somerville
Edited by Nora Shire
Printed in China through Asia Pacific Offset

TO

Ardis (Art) McCasland

Husband

Retired engineer

The bird lady's partner

in avian antics

TABLE OF CONTENTS

Why POOP?

In the fall of 2005, Susanne Reed, publisher of The Big Spring Herald, asked if I would write a column on birds; the purpose of this offering would be educational. After much consideration, I told Susanne that if I did, it would be about the wild, migratory birds my husband, Art, and I have rescued and rehabilitated since 1974.

Holding both state and federal licenses for this work, we realized how significant these birds were to Texas and our nation at various times of the year. Letting the readers know what had happened to the birds, and the outcomes, would be the gist of each week's column.

When I insisted upon calling the column BIRD POOP, Susanne supported me and justified the educational benefits and the name of the column with her staff and corporate headquarters. November of that year was the beginning of the weekly column that is still being offered.

After three years of columns filled with numerous species, I feel that having the columns published in book form will reach even more of an audience. Already well received in our local community, the stories increase awareness of avian wildlife, and appeal to birders, wildlife volunteers, and those who relish seasonal migrations.

BIRD POOP on coffee tables and in the hands of bird lovers throughout the United States is my goal. Since my columns have given information, or poop, relating to the predicaments, efforts of rescue, and final results, perhaps even more birds can be saved.

Hopefully, through a different slant and definition of an oft-used word, the public may become aware of these gifts of nature.

Bebe McCasland

Bebe is federally and state licensed to rehabilitate wild birds.

1. American White Pelican

Pelecanus erythrorhynchos

UNABLE TO CONCEAL HER EXCITEMENT, the teacher's aide greeted my return from lunch with "There's a pelican in your bathroom!"

Numerous songbirds and birds of prey had previously been brought to my office during the noon hour. Some of the birds demanded immediate attention; others were dropped off as a matter of convenience. All could stay in boxes in the bathroom until the end of the school day.

If it had been the fall of the year, I would not have been so amazed. However, it was the third of May. Most of the pelicans migrating

Don Collins

through the Big Spring area were seen on area lakes in October or November. Even stranger was the fact that the pelican had been noticed while walking in front of the abandoned Stuckey's on Interstate-20 west of town. The closest body of water in that area was Four Mile Lake, which parallels the interstate and railroad tracks.

Numerous pelicans rest and feast on the aquatic life in the lake during their fall migration. The pelican's companions had left the lake and continued their journey to the south. For some reason, perhaps this bird stayed in the area, found enough food, and broke its wing as it decided to seek food elsewhere. Another possibility was that it was injured during the spring migration. A passing motorist caught the pelican and delivered it to the school.

One of the largest water birds, with a wingspan of up to nine feet, a pelican can easily eat five pounds of fish a day. With that in mind, my husband Art and I transported the bird to Midge Erskine, who along with husband, Woody, had the Eos Wildlife Sanctuary in Midland. The wing could be set, but the bird would never be able to endure the rigorous flying required during migration. After a lengthy rehab, arrangements were made with the Fort Worth Zoo to accept the pelican.

Leaving early one morning, we drove to Midland to get the bird for its journey to the zoo. Only after staying in quarantine would the pelican be placed with two other non-releasable pelicans with broken wings: one had been found in Grapevine Lake; the other was walking in the middle of the street in downtown Fort Worth. Before we loaded the bird

into a carrier, we noticed it had just swallowed a trout for its morning appetizer. This was to become a real test of our SUV's flow-through ventilation system. The pelican seemed to enjoy the trip, but about Abilene, a distinct aroma filled the vehicle. It seemed with every mile it became more pungent. Partially digested fish may be fine for young pelicans feeding from their mothers' pouches. For us, however, it was a test of our endurance in trying to help wildlife. The zoo was a welcome sight, and their veterinarian immediately took the pelican to the quarantine area.

As we drove back to Big Spring, we felt so privileged to have handled a pelican. Just to hold a wiggling, twenty-five-pound bird with enormous flapping wings and thrashing feet had been a challenge. Little did we know that the following year, in November, another pelican would be found at the same location.

THE ZOO WAS A WELCOME SIGHT, AND THEIR VETERINARIAN IMMEDIATELY TOOK THE PELICAN TO THE QUARANTINE AREA.

2. Greater Roadrunner

Geococcyx californianus

On Christmas Eve, over an hour and a half was spent just trying to get close to a roadrunner in a furniture store. The owner had called that morning. She was concerned that the bird might be hurt and would starve if she could not get it to leave the building. She had left the front door open, but the bird refused to leave.

When Art and I arrived, the paisano was looking out one of the windows. The moment it saw us, it jumped to the floor and was lost in the myriad of sofas, tables, chairs, desks, and end tables. Using a net would be impossible. If we were fortunate enough to grab the bird, our opportunity would be lost if we caught it by the tail. We would have had nothing but a hand full of feathers. Nature has provided this specie with the ability to donate its tail in lieu of capture, either by man or lesser predators.

The bird had a definite advantage — it went under, over, and through furniture at a record clip. Capable of speeds up to twelve to fifteen miles per hour, the roadrunner made us think we might just spend Christmas in that store. Even with the front door open, the bird would turn and run to the back of the store. Although we could see the bird and noticed a limp, we were never close enough to detect exactly what might be wrong with it, except it seemed to love all that furniture.

As we tired of climbing over and around so many items, and made every effort not to break anything, the bird seemed to gain momentum.

Finally, Art suggested that since the bird did not prefer the front of the store, we could try to usher the bird toward the office at the back. If it went in, we could shut the door and have the bird contained.

Fortunately, his idea worked. I squeezed through a slightly opened door, which Art closed behind me. The roadrunner was hiding on a lower shelf of a bookcase. Slowly, I crept toward the bird on hands and knees. I took a deep breath and grabbed at a creature that hardly seemed winded.

Coming out of the office with the captured bird, we noticed it had only one foot. The roadrunner had been leading us on one heck of a chase through all that furniture with one foot and a stub. Where the other foot had been was toughened, scarred skin that had healed over the bottom of the leg.

Ron Alton offered a release site in the Big Spring State Park, and all of us were amazed to see how rapidly the roadrunner disappeared.

SLOWLY, I CREPT TOWARD THE BIRD ON HANDS AND KNEES. I TOOK A DEEP BREATH AND GRABBED...

3. Cedar Waxwing

Bombycilla cedrorum

Inside the shoebox was the familiar sound of bird feet sliding and trying to grip slick cardboard. As I carefully opened the lid for a glimpse, the crested songbird stared back as if I had insulted its privacy. Looking through its facial black mask, the cedar waxwing could only wonder what had happened to its day. Earlier, it had enjoyed a breakfast of mulberries and the companionship of other bandit-looking birds.

"It was in the middle of FM-700. I just knew it'd get hit. So I stopped my car beside it so no one could get close," Margaret Lloyd explained. A lover of any kind of animal life, she had risked her car, her safety, and possibly her sanity to pick up this bird. Margaret added that the cedar waxwing had only one wing.

With the assurance that I would call and let her know the outcome, Margaret left and I immediately examined the bird. Cleanly severed at the shoulder, the wing had left an opening on the side of the bird that enabled me to see inside. This was a new experience. Margaret's use of pressure had stopped the bleeding. Left in the box in a warm, quiet area, the bird had a long shot at surviving such a traumatic injury.

The next morning, I felt the bird must surely have died during the night. It was not to be. The masked marvel once again looked me over, as if demanding breakfast. The only food we had for a bird whose diet included fruit was green grapes, which we diced and offered. Left alone to discover the food and get its bearings, the cedar waxwing ate all the pieces and appeared to feel at home.

As I thought about the injury, I wondered if, in crossing the highway, the bird had hit a car's antenna. Since vessels can spasm and seal when severed this way, I thought perhaps that was the reason it had not bled to death. Two theories about the wound were available: close it; or let the bird's body and nature handle it. We chose the latter.

The next concern, if the waxwing lived, was its diet. Since it was spring, it could feast on the berries of the agarita, a native plant known as red barberry, and fresh mulberries. The weather was suitable for emerging insects, but catching them was a problem. Another "rehabber" suggested PD dog food, which the waxwing accepted if crumbled. During the summer, blueberries and diced grapes could be offered, and in the fall, the berries of the hawthorn, pyracantha, yaupon, juniper, and cedar were available.

Living at a rehab center, the cedar waxwing, nicknamed "Cedi," healed and thrived. It earned its keep for four years by greeting and calming new arrivals. Comfortable in its new environment, it began to trill, and when looking out a window would sometimes offer the characteristic high-pitched whistle of its specie.

As it recovered, the waxwing preened away its disheveled appearance and became the sleek songbird it had been. The bird exemplified its name by its preference for cedar berries and its wing feathers tipped with waxy red droplets. Although its feathers darkened in captivity, they resembled the delicate brush strokes of a master artist.

4. Great Blue Heron

Ardea herodias

As the car approached the top of the viaduct, a long-legged, long-necked bird with a sharp-looking beak was caught in the glare of the headlights. The driver stopped to look at such a strange bird standing in the middle of the road. Glancing both ways to make sure no cars were approaching, the woman slowly eased out of her car and toward the bird. It did not move. Even when she was about a foot away, the bird just stood there, totally unresponsive. If another motorist used the viaduct, he might hit the bird. She decided to put the bird in her car. Then she would figure out what to do with such a bird at nine o'clock in the evening.

When our phone rang, we assumed it was family or a friend calling. A police officer asked if we would come to the police department and get a great blue heron out of the drunk tank. Never having seen the inside of such a holding facility, we knew this would be a new experience. As the officer led us to the enclosure, he explained that since an animal control officer was not available at that hour, the heron had been placed in the empty tank. He added that he was concerned about getting an occupant at any time.

As the officer opened the steel door we could see the motionless heron. We easily picked up the bird, which offered no resistance, and placed it in a carrier. The officer thanked us for removing the bird before any inebriated person had to be placed in the tank. We could imagine what the bird and the drunk might have thought of each other.

Once home, we examined the heron. There were no visible injuries, but the beak, feet, and feathers were characteristic of older birds. The toes were missing from one foot. Its lethargy was troubling. Fortunately for the woman and the officer, the heron was not young and energetic. The bird, with its spear-like beak, would have defensively struck at the eyes, and was capable of piercing one's skull. Once an expert at fishing, the heron would have stood in the shallow water of a lake, pond, river, or creek, absolutely still, head poised and ready, waiting for a fish to swim into the shadows cast by its body. At the right moment, the heron would have grabbed its aquatic meal in the razor-sharp edges of its beak.

The grey-blue heron had flown its last migration. Its large, slow-moving wings could take it no further. To us, it was a lesson in the inevitable.

THE OFFICER THANKED US FOR REMOVING THE BIRD BEFORE ANY INEBRIATED PERSON HAD TO BE PLACED IN THE TANK.

5. Ferruginous Hawk

Buteo regalis

The caller's concern for a bird trapped in the abandoned control tower at our local airpark was genuine. "It's an owl and can't get out. It keeps crashing into the windows. I'm afraid it'll hurt itself or starve," she said. Telling her I'd call her back as soon as I talked to the manager of the airpark, I learned that he had seen owls coming and going from the tower, since the panes of many windows in the stairwell were missing. He felt the bird would be able to leave due to the open access from the bottom to the top. When I returned the call of the Western Container employee, I related that I had talked to the manager, and agreed with him that owls are notorious for getting into and out of structures. I asked her to call if she saw the bird strike the windows again. My husband and I drove out to the tower several times, but no bird was visible. Only pigeons were availing themselves of this five-story birdhouse.

A few days later the woman called to say the owl was still in the top of the tower. She had been out of town, and upon returning to work had seen the bird flying into the windows. Once again, I called the manager; we agreed to meet at the tower to check on the bird. As Art and I drove toward the north side of the tower, I could clearly see the silhouette of a large hawk.

As the manager walked up to meet us, I informed him of a major problem. "That's not an owl. It's a hawk. It cannot get out of the tower." An owl could figure out how to leave. A hawk is a straight, open-field flier and would never find an exit. Unlocking the door, the manager waited to greet the game warden, who had just arrived. Art and I carefully started up the metal steps, which were coated with dried pigeon droppings and feathers. The final approach to the top floor, where controllers had instructed thousands of student pilots, was extremely steep. As we entered the control part of the tower, the hawk spotted us and flew into the windows. Badly discolored, the windows were covered with the effects of numerous birds that had tried to escape. Unable to gain flight speed, the hawk did not impact the windows with enough force to hurt itself.

Above the entrance to the control room was a narrow space leading to the top of the structure. A door to the roof had been left open. The hawk could have been pursuing a pigeon, and followed it down the opening and into the control room. This very large ferruginous hawk had managed to stay alive by catching pigeons.

With net in hand, I watched as the hawk flew from one side to the other. The span of its wings was almost six feet. Time and again, it flew, only to hit the windows. Able to put a net over it, I pressed it to the window which allowed it to slide onto the controller's console. As I caught its legs and had its feet under control, Art removed the net. By the time the manager and game warden finished their climb into the control area, the bird was secure and ready to be placed in a carrier. We explained how grateful we were for being allowed to enter the structure; the hawk would never have escaped.

After our climb down, we met the lady who had made the phone calls. She was heartily thanked for her persistence because she was instrumental in saving the hawk's life.

6. SANDHILL CRANE
Grus canadensis

IN THE SEEMINGLY ENDLESS PLOWED fields, the solitary crane walked slowly across the mounds while looking for insects and mice. Occasionally it probed its strong beak into the ground for earthworms. Having alerted us about an injured sandhill crane, a farmer added that a family of cranes came each morning and stayed with the bird until late afternoon. Then the flock would fly to a safer place to spend the night. It was only a matter of time before coyotes found the bird.

To catch a crane in open fields seemed impossible, but six volunteers joined me in the attempt. Bob Parker and his son, Mike Parker, and Jerry Parnell were given a thirty-two-foot net and assigned to the south. If the bird headed their way, they would become a human fence line in trying to slow the crane until we could catch it. With me were Midge and Woody Erskine, who ran the Eos Wildlife Sanctuary in Midland, and John Petty, an energetic young man who had been involved in other rescues.

As we approached the crane, it headed north. With its long legs, the bird easily walked on the mounds and was gaining distance from us while we stepped over the mounds rather than sink into them. Running, then walking, the crane finally came to an unplowed field with a fenced enclosure. The bird effortlessly stepped through the four-strand barbed wire fence, walked across a grassy area, and through another fence. To go around this enclosed pasture would take too much time and allow the crane to get farther away. So into the area we went. Only when we were inside did we notice the bull and realize we were in a bull pen.

Looking up from eating, the animal glared at us, swished its tail, but seemed content to allow us to walk slowly toward the opposite fence. Just climbing through the barbed wire had slowed our progress in getting closer to the bird. John volunteered to run ahead of the crane and make it turn back towards us. That ploy worked, and the bird headed back to the south and us. As it approached, however, it veered, outmaneuvered us, and crossed back into the bull pen again. The Erskines chose to go around the pen this time, but John and I were so close to the bird we did not want to lose our advantage. He held the wire as we reentered the bull's domain.

With humans interfering with his realm, the bull snorted and started to paw the ground.

Running across the field might have caused the bull to attack. Instead, we walked and hoped we could get to the other side without causing this beast to take drastic measures. As John went through the fence, and I climbed over it, the bull charged. Fortunately, we were on the other side and running again.

By this time, the sandhill had decided to move west with the four of us in pursuit. Suddenly, it decided to head east, toward the bull pen, and coyote fencing, which we had not noticed previously. If we could run it into that, we had a chance at capturing it. The crane seemed confused by a fence that offered no opening. This was the break we needed. The four of us ran toward the bird, with John to the north and Woody to the south. Midge and I were neck and neck as we approached the

RUNNING, THEN WALKING, THE CRANE FINALLY CAME TO AN UNPLOWED FIELD WITH A FENCED ENCLOSURE...

crane. When she suddenly disappeared, I turned to see that she had tripped over a mound and was lying face down in the dirt. With only ten feet to go, and with my last amount of energy, I reached the crane and grabbed its beak as it still tried to go through the fence. Behind me Midge was yelling, "Watch the beak!" I had the beak in my right hand, and my left arm was wrapped around the angry bird's wings and body. What I did not expect were its sharp-clawed toes trying to run up my leg. John quickly grabbed the flailing feet, and we had "the impossible." The four of us stood in the field for several minutes as we caught our breath and felt our hearts resume their normal beat. We figured we had run and walked over a mile and a half of plowed land.

The Erskines took the crane; the prognosis was good. The wing could be set, and the last time we saw the crane, it was enjoying the company of two other sandhills in the backyard of their sanctuary.

BEHIND ME MIDGE WAS YELLING, "WATCH THE BEAK!" I HAD THE BEAK IN MY RIGHT HAND, AND MY LEFT ARM WAS WRAPPED AROUND THE ANGRY BIRD'S WINGS AND BODY.

7. Pied-billed Grebe

Podilymbus podiceps

In our hands, the small duck-like bird mesmerized us with its delicate beauty. The luster of its soft feathers was remarkable. Nature had to have had a sense of humor in painting a black band around the center of its short beak. Although we had handled an eared grebe, this was our first pied-billed, which is considered one of the best swimmers among aquatic birds.

Mistaking asphalt for water as it migrated on a moonlit night, the grebe had landed on wet pavement rather than on a nearby shallow pond. With its lobed toes, the pied-billed had great difficulty moving or walking. It also had a need similar to the loon to run on a watery surface in order to become airborne. Knowing that this bird lived, fed, and courted on water, we had to return it to nature as soon as possible. To make sure it could swim, we placed it in our bathtub, and watched to make sure the legs and feet were doing their job. From one end of the tub to the other, the pied-billed paddled and seemed eager for a larger pond.

An area lake was selected for the bird's release. The aquatic insects and small fish needed for its diet would be abundant. Walking along the shoreline, we searched for an area away from human activity and where the water had some depth. Placed on the surface of the water, the grebe instantly deflated and sank out of sight. My husband asked if we had done the wrong thing. "It drowned. We drowned that bird," he lamented. From the dusty regions of my mind, I reminded him of an article I had read about pied-billed grebes. These unique birds, when frightened or in danger, would rapidly release air from their feathers and body, sink below the surface, and swim far enough away to resurface and continue their escape. We waited. Almost thirty seconds elapsed. Then the surface of the lake rippled. The little grebe was with us again.

Since that day, a variety of grebes have arrived from as far away as Pecos, Odessa, and Snyder, and as close as our Big Spring State Hospital, north of town, and the Big Spring Refinery. Each time we have marveled at the feet on these birds. They may not be able to walk well, but those creatively formed lobes enable them to propel themselves through the water with great speed. Because of their short tails, the grebes also extend their feet behind their bodies in order to steer themselves in flight. With the release of many more grebes, we never again experienced one that dropped to the bottom like a rock.

8. Great Horned Owl

Bubo virginianus

Sitting on a siding, the train crew heard sleet hitting the windows when the late winter storm arrived. Soon the mesquites and grasses were encased in an eerie opaque glaze. The crew's day had been one of frustration, with problems up and down the line. It seemed the go-ahead to reenter the main line would never come.

Finally given the green light to proceed, the locomotive surged to life with its cargo in tow. Far ahead, barely visible in the headlight, was something standing in the middle of the tracks. Accustomed to seeing bobcats, foxes, and coyotes saunter across the tracks, the crew had even seen rattlesnakes coiled between the rails. This thing, however, did not move. To continue meant the engine would hit it.

Since they had moved only a few yards, the engineer stopped the train and gave the order to investigate the object. By this time the storm had coated everything with ice; the crewman had difficulty in opening the door of the cab. Carefully leaving the slick ladder on the side of the train, the man started walking and slipping toward the dark image down the tracks. Even as he broke through the ice and crunched in the ballast, the shape did not move. When he was finally close enough to see it clearly, he discovered it was a large great horned owl, which had probably landed between the tracks as it hunted for prey.

Once down, the bird had huddled against the icy blasts of the storm. It had taken very little time for the moisture accompanying the sleet to adhere to the bird's feathers. The weight of the ice had prevented the owl from seeking refuge away from the tracks.

Because the owl had not flown away as he approached, the man hoped it was still alive and not frozen. Taking off his coat, he wrapped it around the bird and brought it back to the engine. Once inside, the crewman removed the coat. He and the engineer could detect movement in the owl's chest. It was still breathing. They placed the bird in a box for the trip into town.

By the time we received the great horned owl, some of the ice had melted, but remnants still coated the wing feathers and parts of its head. The crew wondered if there would be any lasting effects from the ice. We told them the ice could very well have saved the bird's life because it provided additional insulation as protection from the storm. The crew's alertness in spotting the bird, and their efforts in helping it, had been a major factor in the bird's survival.

After several days of recovery and well-supplied with mice and rabbits, the owl was released one evening during a week of good weather.

HE AND THE ENGINEER COULD DETECT MOVEMENT IN THE OWL'S CHEST. IT WAS STILL BREATHING...

9. Turkey Vulture

Cathartes aura

After a stop for coffee in Sterling City, the Department of Public Safety (DPS) officers drove north to patrol the lonely, dark stretch of road to Big Spring. When they were nearly five miles from town, their headlights illuminated a car parked in the grass beside the road.

Nearing the vehicle, one officer relayed the license number while the other parked behind the faded Camaro. It appeared the only occupant of the car was the driver, who had slumped forward onto the steering wheel. Leaving their cruiser, the DPS officers cautiously approached the car.

The first officer's flashlight wandered upon a young man in his mid-twenties. Noticing that both windows were down on the driver's side, the officer was concerned about how unprotected the driver was. Several steps behind, and on the other side of the car, his partner noted that the back window was down. As he reached the door and his flashlight shone on the front passenger seat, he gasped as he quickly stepped backward. Hearing his partner's voice, the first officer saw his reaction.

Suddenly the still night air was pierced with laughter. In the front seat and looking from one officer to the other, a turkey vulture had turned apprehension into uncontrollable giggles.

Roused by the chuckling of the officers, the young man awoke. When asked about his passenger, he told them he had found the bird by the side of the road as he left San Antonio. When he discovered it could not fly, he put it in his car rather than leave it to be hit. Sitting quietly beside him, the vulture had seemed to enjoy the ride and had used the floor mat for his droppings.

Since the man was obviously weary from his long drive, the officers suggested they follow him into town. They also informed him that the vulture was state and federally protected; they would notify the game warden to locate the nearest rehabilitation facility.

When our phone rang at 10:45 p.m., we told the officers we could meet them in five minutes, since they were parked at the old Wal-Mart. To see the red-headed bird of prey sitting in the front seat of an automobile was the most comical situation we had had with vultures. Assuring the young man and the officers that the bird would receive care, and thanking all involved in the bird's journey, we took this carrion-eater home.

After examining a wing that had an old break with much calcification, we put the vulture in a carrier in our den for the night. At the other end of the house, I soon learned why the young man had lowered three of four windows in his car. The aroma of regurgitated skunk filled the house. Accustomed to being outdoors, the vulture spent the rest of the night outside. Although non-releasable, the vulture would live to spend its days as an educational specimen of nature's method of recycling.

10. RED-SHOULDERED HAWK

Buteo lineatus

As the broad-winged hawk soared over the town and countryside, it enjoyed the rising current of a January afternoon. Unseasonably warm weather encouraged the immature bird to take advantage of each thermal (a rising body of warm air). Suddenly its left wing was jolted by an unseen object and searing pain. No longer could that wing give the bird freedom of flight.

Descending rapidly, the hawk fought to control its landing. Impacting an area with loose dirt and gravel, the bird gasped. The dust was irritating to its lungs and eyes. As it lay on the ground, the hawk tried to get its bearings. The next moment it was lifted, carried, and dropped into a large dark place. As the hawk hit the bottom, its talons dug into a thick, sticky substance. Looking up at the sky, and trying to figure out where it was, the bird saw its afternoon shut off by more black, which met the sides of wherever it was. The odors of this strange place were unpleasant, and the only light the bird could see was an overhead streak of blue in the middle of all the darkness. The bird's day had turned into night.

As a young man opened his back gate, he gathered several bags of trash to put in the dumpster. When he raised the lid, something moved. Dropping the lid and jumping backwards, he could not imagine what could be in there. The city had emptied the container the previous day. Slowly lifting the lid, he glanced inside and saw a large bird standing in a corner. The hawk wanted to take this opportunity to leave, but could not fly. Realizing that someone had put an injured bird in an empty dumpster, the man called Animal Control.

When the lid to the dumpster was raised again, the hawk saw an unusual object coming toward it. The bird tried to evade the net, but the officer was able to snare it and hand it to a fellow officer. Upon seeing the hawk, the young man told them he had seen a bird like that flying around the neighborhood for the last two weeks. Thanking him, they took it to the Andrews Veterinary Clinic.

Calling from the clinic, an employee said they had a red-tailed hawk. When we arrived, we approached the outdoor cage where the veterinarian had placed the bird. Smaller than a red-tailed, and not having the familiar markings, the bird had a nondescript coloration except for the streaks of brown running from its upper chest to its legs. Although we were not familiar with this specie, we knew it was definitely an immature hawk and were eager to examine it. After climbing into the cage and grabbing the hawk, I extended its left wing. "This hawk's been shot," I told my husband. We both could feel the hard substance that was imbedded in the outer part of the wing.

The next day, the hawk and I visited with Dr. Scott Burt, a Big Spring veterinarian. Confirming that the bird had been shot, he could not detect any major breakage of bones. After he gave it injections to counter swelling and infection, Dr. Burt agreed this hawk should be taken to the South Plains Rehabilitation Center in Lubbock.

Debbie Tennyson, center manager, identified the bird as a red-shouldered hawk. Only as an adult would the hawk have the reddish patches on each shoulder. As we related the story and ordeal of this creature, Debbie asked more than once, "Where did you say you got this bird?" Her questions were well-founded.

With its vast arid plains, Andrews, Texas, is red-tailed hawk country. Normally, red-shouldered hawks are not in the same locale. They frequent forested areas, nest high in trees, and hunt in swampy river bottoms and along heavily wooded creek beds. While both species prey upon mice, rabbits, and skunks, the red-shouldered hawk also appreciates tree squirrels, toads, frogs, turtles, even snails and earthworms.

Since the young man in Andrews said he thought he had seen the hawk flying over his neighborhood, we could imagine it had perhaps been "somebody's bird." Possession of any wild migratory bird would violate federal and state law. Migration was another possibility. Whatever the circumstances, the hawk had been a victim of unconscionable cruelty.

An X-ray of the wound confirmed a pellet, plus a tiny bone fracture. The rehab center's veterinarians decided to leave the pellet in the wing. Too much damage would occur if the pellet were removed. After several weeks of confinement for the wing to heal, the hawk was placed in a mew for exercise. Fully recovered from its injury, it is now in the large flight cage and flies effortlessly. During the Easter weekend, the red-shouldered hawk will be released in the Hill Country of central Texas. From a dumpster to freedom, it had a remarkable journey.

11. BLACK-CHINNED HUMMINGBIRD

Archilochus alexandri

Like a swarm of bees, carpenters, electricians, and plumbers descended upon the stately home. From the piles of supplies outside, it was obvious that a major renovation had begun. Inside, the vintage house had been gutted. Although the original craftsmen had constructed a lasting testament to their skills, age had compromised wiring and plumbing. While retaining and enhancing this architectural beauty of the late 1930s, the owner was adamant about modernizing the home of her parents.

As spring turned into summer, renovation continued with a constant stream of deliveries.

Workmen walked back and forth to grab yet another tool or some material from their trucks. The craftsmen had come to know each other even though their expertise differed.

As a carpenter headed home one afternoon, he stopped to talk with an electrician who was pulling heavy wire through a hole in the overhang of the roof. Although the recessed lighting for the outside of the house had been delayed, the wiring could be completed, with the fixture to be installed later. Putting a loop in the wire to keep it from being pulled back into the attic, the electrician was finished for the day. He was glad to leave because the west side of the house was the hottest.

A few weeks later, the owner was walking through the house to see how the renovation was progressing. Looking out a bathroom window, she noticed the looped wire. Nestled inside was a cup-like woven structure. The outside appeared to be coated with a silky substance. Lichen from the bark of trees was evident. Unsure of what she was seeing, the lady suddenly noticed a movement at the top of the little cup. A slender pointed bill emerged, followed by the small green-above, white-below body of a female hummingbird.

After the bird's mate had dominated this nesting area, he left her with the promise of offspring, and available food for herself and their young. Only she would gather spider webs, plant down and lichen for her nest, and feed them.

Fascinated by the bird and the possibility of baby hummingbirds, the lady spent as much time as possible watching the nest. A little over two weeks later, the mother bird started flying back and forth to the nest throughout the day. The eggs had hatched.

Over the next three weeks, the hummingbird's swift flight brought food to her young. She used the lady's flowerbeds as well as the neighbors' yards to find nectar and insects. Flies, gnats, mosquitoes, aphids, and spiders were no match for her hunting abilities. As the nestlings grew, their nest expanded with them because of the elasticity of the spiders' silk.

When our friend first noticed the nest, she called us to come and enjoy such a close view of nature. She instructed the workmen to stay away from that part of the house. We advised that as long as no people were allowed in the area, the black-chinned hummer should probably continue to raise her family. Only if something unforeseen happened would we intervene in this wonderful experience.

Finally, the day came when the young made their first venture from the nest. Nearby shrubs and trees offered good cover while the fledglings depended upon their mother for food.

Fortunately, during the frenzied activity involved in renovating the home, no one, except the thoughtful owner, noticed what this delicate creature had accomplished. Relieved that no rescue or intervention was necessary, we were privileged to witness both the bird's renewal of nature and the owner's restoration of a quiet elegance to her neighborhood.

12. Chimney Swifts

Chaetura pelagica

The nest vibrated with the sudden clap of thunder. The hatchlings nestled against each other for reassurance, while their mother clung to the side of the nest. Preceded by flashes of light, the thunder increased. When the rain began, it fell softly. In a matter of minutes, a spring shower suddenly turned into a torrent of water.

As droplets of moisture pelted the mother and her babies, the nest shook and was dislodged. Tumbling downwards, it struck objects that jolted the family that depended upon it. Coming to an abrupt halt, the contents of their cup-shaped home were scattered.

Arriving early the next day at the Potton House, a turn-of-the-century home, the volunteer expected the worst from the early morning storm. Grabbing towels, she immediately went to the fireplace. Every time a hard rain occurred, the chimney leaked and water would be on the floor.

As she turned the corner and proceeded into the room, she stopped. On the floor with the puddle of water was what appeared to be a wet baby mouse. Taking a towel, she scooped it up and placed it aside. After removing the decorative fireplace screen, she discovered three more mice. As one of them moved, she was startled to discover that they were not mice after all. The four gray, helpless babies were birds.

When we arrived, the volunteer had wrapped the babies in a cloth and was trying to keep them warm. The chimney swifts would be quite a challenge.

As we examined the fireplace, we saw the mother bird leave the damper area and retreat up the chimney. Bravely, she had stayed with her young, even though they had been strewn across the hearth. Due to the water coursing down the chimney during the storm, the nest had been loosened from the bricks. In building the stick nest, which was held together and to the chimney wall with her saliva, the mother's efforts had been successful. The nest protected her offspring through the ride of their lives.

Once home, we devised a makeshift nest to resemble their former home. Their toes immediately grabbed the rough sides. The birds seemed contented. A diet of formula and insects was readily accepted. Pinfeathers emerged quickly. Feathers unfurled. Eyes opened.

With their forward-facing toes and tail feathers tipped with spines, the maturing swifts would be able to cling to any vertical surface.

At this stage of development, the swifts were ready for the wildlife center. We thought about returning them to the Potton House chimney, but could not be sure the mother or an adult bird would assume responsibility. The swifts would take flight in a special area at the center.

Most memorable would be our daily handling of the swifts. It would be hard to forget their climbing our arms during numerous daily feedings, and their twittering conversations. Our job was done.

13. Red-tailed Hawks
Buteo jamaicensis

WITH HIS HAT PULLED DOWN TIGHT against the wind, the rancher rode his horse to the far north pasture of the ranch. As he reached a plateau in the rocky hills, the screams were audible in spite of the strong gusts of spring. Above, two hawks were battling the weather to reach a telephone pole. The rider guessed the birds were beginning their March courtship. Around the first of April, the rancher decided to check the pasture for any signs of a nest.

He was well acquainted with the aerial displays of red-tailed hawks. Over the years he

had seen the female turn in flight to extend her talons toward the approaching mate. Familiar with their vocal callings, he anticipated watching a new family emerge.

Sure enough, on that same pole where he had seen the birds in March, there was a large nest of sticks and twigs. The female was nestled inside. Knowing the male would feed her during incubation, the rider made a note that the eggs would probably hatch about the first of May.

Delayed by spring roundup, the rancher returned in late May to check on the hawks and their young. With his binoculars, he could see two nestlings with their white chests streaked with brown. They were anticipating their mother's return. She would bring them a cottontail, or maybe a rat or snake.

As the female hawk approached with a rabbit in her talons, the nestlings moved toward the edge of the nest. Trying to drop her prey beside the babies, the mother used one foot to grab at a part of the transformer. As the rabbit fell from her other foot, the tip of her wing touched a line. Going through her body, the surge of electricity caused the parent to tumble to the ground.

Still astride his horse, the rancher could not believe what he had seen through his binoculars. As he slumped in the saddle and lowered his head, a tear ran down his cheek.

After a few moments, he slowly rode his horse to the pole where the mother lay face down in the grass. Noticeable was the chestnut red of her tail. Dismounting, he walked over to the hawk. Gently picking her up, he noticed the familiar broad band of dark streaks across her white belly. He'd always thought of it as a cummerbund, a distinct marking for such a noble raptor.

STILL ASTRIDE HIS HORSE, THE RANCHER COULD NOT BELIEVE WHAT HE HAD SEEN THROUGH HIS BINOCULARS...

As he regained his composure, he realized something had to be done for the two youngsters high above him. Remounting, he rode as fast as he safely could back to the ranch headquarters. Calling the game warden, he started a race for time in saving the hawks.

"A ranch outside of Sweetwater" was the location given to us by the game warden. The electric company was contacted, but it would take a few days. "We don't have a few days," was our reply. Whether the male hawk would feed the nestlings was questionable. The weather report for the next three days was for daytime temperatures to be in the 100s. We waited.

The morning of the third day the game warden called to say the equipment was on the ranch and headed toward the pole to rescue the hawks. Over rough terrain, the crew drove around brush and cactus that had covered the road once bladed when the poles were installed. About 1:00 p.m., the warden called with good news as he drove toward Big Spring. The men had taken the young hawks from the nest.

The nestlings were treated for dehydration, because most of their intake of moisture comes from their food. When we started them on beef heart and mice, it was obvious they were ravenous. Because of the rancher, a game warden, and the electric company, the young red-tails would grow up to soar, hunt, and enjoy a lifelong mate in a territory they would claim year after year.

"WE DON'T HAVE A FEW DAYS," WAS OUR REPLY. WHETHER THE MALE HAWK WOULD FEED THE NESTLINGS WAS QUESTIONABLE.

14. HOUSE FINCHES

Carpodacus mexicanus

When the doorbell rang, it was another announcement of "baby season." The young boy, with hands cupped together, stood beside his mother. Slowly, he carefully exposed the baby birds he had found in his yard. Bald, sightless, and totally helpless, the nestlings were warm and moist from the boy's hands. They appeared to be two to three days old.

As the boy related how he had found each bird nestled in their grass, the mother added that she could not figure out how they came to be in that location. "They could not have fallen out of a nest, since there's no tree in our front yard." Telling her they had probably been transported to that spot, I mentioned that grackles are notorious for robbing nests of eggs and the newly born. Once they have a nestling, they land in hopes of having a meal. Frightened by a person or cat, the large bird departs while leaving the baby to fend for itself. To have three babies may have meant there was more than one culprit in the kidnapping of these birds.

The tedious, time-consuming effort to feed the tiny ones began. From dawn to dusk, every thirty minutes, the young were given formula. As the sparrow-like birds grew, the time of feeding stretched to forty-five minutes. Unable to duplicate their mother's offering of dandelion seeds, we supplemented with moistened cat pellets and fruit. From their voices we could tell they were house finches.

Even though the nestlings were now about eight days old, they would have to travel with me when I made a scheduled trip to San Angelo to take my mother to the doctor. The day of our trip, my regular transportation presented too many problems to be on the highway. My husband and I had bought a Porsche; it would have to get us there and back.

Leaving Big Spring with the three babies, their food, and mom, I headed south. To drive the sports car was a thrill, and my mother was excited. "It's such a fun experience," she said on every occasion that the low-built car took to the road.

While she visited with her doctor, I kept going out to the car to feed my young brood.

As we left the parking lot and headed toward U.S. 87 and home, I anticipated the enjoyment of 85 miles of driving the Porsche almost as much as Mom looked forward to the shifting of gears and the purr of the engine.

Shifting from first to second while turning onto Knickerbocker, I felt the tremendous vibration in the stick shift at the same time the "ka-blam!" signaled a major problem. Unable to shift into anything but fifth gear, I told Mom to hang on, because if I didn't make every traffic light, we'd be in San Angelo for a while.

The next to the last signal light caught us. We could no longer cruise at the necessary speed to stay in fifth gear. Pulling over to the curb at a fast-food restaurant, I took Mom and my charges inside. After they were settled in a booth, I begged two employees to help me push the car into their parking lot. Then I called my husband.

Still at the refinery, Art was distraught over anything happening to the Porsche. My description of the clutch problem was frightening. He would have to tow us home. Finishing his work at the plant, he gathered what was necessary. It would take at least an hour and a half to two hours before he arrived.

Meanwhile, the birds had to be fed. Since I had put the babies in a large tote for their trip, they didn't seem to mind being carried to the Ladies

Room every forty-five minutes. After eating, they would settle down and be quiet until hungry again.

Finally, Art appeared. The ride back to Big Spring had a stop in Sterling City for the birds' last feeding. By that time, the heat of the day was noticeable. Not only did my husband endure a very warm Porsche as I towed him home; he also had lots of time to worry about what had happened to his beloved car.

To learn that metal fatigue had caused the failure of our clutch plate was a relief. At least it wasn't my driving. Thanking the young men who had helped my little car, we sent them a monetary gift as well as a letter to corporate headquarters. The "Golden Arches" will always remind me of an unintended stay and the smell of French fries.

Two of the three house finches developed a male's bright-red head, breast, and rump of adulthood. The female became less conspicuous in a drab costume of gray-brown with grayish streaks down the front of her body. They were a welcome addition to our neighborhood.

15. Mississippi Kites

Ictinia mississippiensis

The game warden's voice conveyed the seriousness of a situation on the east side of town. With summer months we are accustomed to concerns about baby birds and nests. However, the relentless pursuit of any perceived threat by Mississippi kites has to be handled both for the sake of the birds and those confronting feathered aggression.

Having spent their winters as far south as Argentina, the hawks returned to take advantage of the abundant food source in our area. Since the kite is quite adroit at catching insects in flight, cicadas, grasshoppers, and dragonflies are easy prey.

Extremely aggressive in defense of their young, the kites, without warning, will sometimes "dive-bomb" dogs, postmen, and anyone in their territory. Such was happening at this particular home.

"A man has told his neighbors he's going to shoot the birds. Every time he goes out his front door, a kite swoops down at him." I asked the warden to inform the man that as soon as I left work, I would come and get the babies and destroy the nest. Giving us the leeway to make this decision, the U. S. Fish & Wildlife Service realizes that some situations warrant intervention.

During early afternoon, the warden called again. "Get over there as soon as you can. This morning, one of the kites cut the man's head. With his drinking problem, he's liable to shoot up the whole neighborhood."

While standing on his front porch and telling him exactly what I would be doing, I noticed there were no menacing hawks attacking us. Showing me a small scratch on the upper part of his forehead, the man had given no attention to the cleaning of his cut. As he displayed the faint line of dried blood, I could readily detect the lingering aroma of alcohol on his breath.

In the front yard, the mulberry tree presented quite a climb. About three feet from the top, and sheltered under a dense growth of leaves, was the nest. My luck was holding. The only way one of the parents could reach me was from below. Gathering the two nestlings, I placed them in a pillowcase, which I then secured below my chin. Destroying the nest was an effort, in that the kite had interwoven sticks in a triangular fork of the tree.

As I started to climb down from my perch some thirty feet above the ground, I heard a siren in the distance. The alarm grew louder and closer.

Suddenly, a squad car from the west, and the game warden's truck from the east, skidded to a stop on the street gravel and dirt under the tree. Both officers rushed out of their cars to the man who, unknown to me, was standing at the base of the tree.

During my climb, descent, and the man's entrance on the scene, a neighbor had witnessed only the man looking up in the tree. Afraid he would finally carry out his threat because he had been seen numerous times near the tree, she called the police to come as quickly as possible.

Finally on the ground, I showed the youngsters to the man who seemed satisfied that the hawks would quit harassing him. After he had gone back into his house, I asked the officers what had happened. "We were told he had a gun. We thought he might shoot you as well as the birds."

16. Burrowing Owl

Athene cunicularia

On the recorder was a message from the manager of the Big Spring State Park. After he retrieved a young burrowing owl that a lady had found at the airpark, he would bring the bird to us.

Upon arrival, Ron Alton told about meeting a tourist in the park that morning. She was from Houston. Since she wanted to see prairie dogs and burrowing owls, he had given her directions to the best location within the airpark for viewing these species.

As the Houstonian slowly drove by the burrows as the "dogs" and owls were sunning after the previous evening's storm and hard rain, she noticed a young owl lying on the ground some distance from the closest hole. Recognizing that this was out of the norm, she called Ron for assistance.

"How she saw that small owl on the ground is beyond me! Their coloration blends so well with the terrain, it would be almost impossible to see the owl." As he handed the bird to me, he added, "I hope you can save it."

Listless, with a very cool body temperature and damp to the touch, the little owl had probably suffered a very traumatic night. Away from its mother, caught out in the storm, it had somehow withstood the downpour. Thank-ing Ron for the delivery and turning to go inside, I slipped the bird inside my shirt.

With one hand holding the owl against my midriff, I had an instant transfer of body heat to the small creature. Faster than waiting for an incubator to gain the preferred temperature, the procedure worked. As Art came from another room, he saw my Napoleonic stance, and sighed, "What do you have this time?"

Even when the burrowing owl was warm and dry, it was weak from its ordeal and could not stand. Mincing a baby mouse, since it may not have been fed the night before, I opened its beak and slowly put small bits into its throat. Although relieved to see that it swallowed readily, I knew the owl and I weren't out of the woods yet.

Bedraggled feathers were nothing compared to the mud on the owl's beak, legs, and talons. Slowly, we were able to remove the dirt from its mouth and feet. With the movement of its legs as it resisted handling, the remaining soil came off like fine talcum powder. Of concern was the owl's right eye which remained closed. Perhaps it had flown into something or been slammed to the ground by a wind gust.

Late that day, with one baby mouse for fuel, the burrowing owl stood. Another minced mouse was given after dark. The next morning, the bird greeted us with the right eye half-open. Since it was too weak to tear its food, we continued mincing its meals and giving it plenty to eat.

The third day, the owl's eye was completely open. Having gained strength and confidence, the bird was ready for a larger container with a hidey-hole (a hideaway). Unable to duplicate a burrow, we fashioned a place for the bird to hide within a small cardboard box. Each time we approached the owl's domain, it would run and hide in what it considered a safe home.

With several resident burrowing owls, the wildlife center in Lubbock was the next stop for the bird. The week that followed was one of progress. The little owl was tearing its food and eating on its own. In the company of other owls, it was acting normal. Soon it graduated to a mew where it could fly, catch, and kill live food. It was ready for placement and taken to a developing colony of burrowing owls and prairie dogs in Mitchell County.

17. Mississippi Kite

Ictinia mississippiensis

By late August, the young had left the nest. Soaring on a rising thermal with their parents high above the neighborhood, the juvenile Mississippi kites were fortunate enough to have been born during early summer. They would be ready to migrate in September.

Having two nests that needed to be destroyed, the game warden notified us of the locations. The homeowners had been willing to tolerate the daily dive-bombings of parent kites. Knowing that as soon as the young left the nest the attacks would cease, the residents had been very cooperative in working with the warden and the birds. In both cases, the adult birds had been exceedingly aggressive in defense of their young.

While some kites display such actions, others do not. Since the birds might use the same nests the following year, the warden felt the best solution to this problem was the removal of the nests once the young had left the area. Our state and federal licenses allow such action.

Without Art to help, I asked my friend and co-worker, Lupe Urias, for assistance one afternoon. With public schools in session and adults at work,

we anticipated the neighborhoods would be quiet, and our work quickly completed.

Loading both a tall stepladder and an extension ladder in Lupe's truck, we headed to the north side of town. Between the home and a local restaurant was a vacant lot with a dead elm tree. The kites had built their nest in an area where the tree branched into three large limbs. From that location the parent birds could easily see when a lady came out her front door and crossed the porch to reach her car. The kites considered it a threat. Daily, they had flown through the porch and tried to scare the woman. They succeeded.

Our suggestion had been to confuse the kites by carrying an umbrella. Soon they remained at the nest site whenever the lady had used her parasol to access her car. For weeks the routine continued. Then one day she noticed the nest was empty.

Having removed that nest, Lupe and I drove to the east side of town. A large mulberry tree had been the home for a kite family for several years. The parents never ceased in their war on the homeowner. Lupe helped me unload the stepladder and held it while I climbed to the nest and removed it. After picking up the debris, we secured the ladders and left.

During the drive home, I looked at our attire. Not knowing what we would encounter, we both had dressed for the worse. We were glad the neighborhoods were nearly deserted and our job easy.

That evening I told Art of our adventures. Of special interest was the woman on the north side. In our many years of bird rescue and rehab, we had met people of different racial, ethnic, economic and social backgrounds. Our work had introduced us to people from many countries and with many dialects. The language of birds, however, seemed a common thread. The woman, who had taken the time to learn about kites and was willing to understand the circumstances from the birds' point of view, was one of the most notable ladies I ever met.

At the refinery the next morning, an employee stopped Art in the hallway. The man was very upset at the fact that some Mexicans had parked across the street from his house. They had brought ladders, and destroyed the kite's nest. Trying to explain what is allowed in the case of aggressive birds, Art was interrupted several times by the person who was so upset about two Mexicans removing that nest. As Art started to return to his office, the man stated he understood why the nest was destroyed. He just didn't like those Mexicans coming into his neighborhood and doing it. When the man had finished, Art calmly replied, "One of those Mexicans was my wife."

THE KITES CONSIDERED IT A THREAT. DAILY, THEY HAD FLOWN THROUGH THE PORCH AND TRIED TO SCARE THE WOMAN. THEY SUCCEEDED.

18. Peregrine Falcon — "Emperor"

Falco peregrinus

Dove season had opened before Labor Day that year. On the drive back to Big Spring, two hunters talked about their day and the birds they had bagged. One of the men decided that he would call us regarding a floundering red-tailed hawk they had seen near their pickup as they prepared to come home.

Since hunters sometimes find injured birds during an outing, we were not surprised to receive a call that evening. "Would you like to go with us tomorrow to see if we can find that hawk?" asked the hunter. "We left several doves for it to eat since we knew it couldn't fly." My reply was first to thank them for leaving food for the bird. Meeting them the next morning would be great, since they would be using part of their Labor Day holiday to look for a hawk that might or might not be found

Heading northwest on the highway to Andrews, we passed miles of open country, patches of mesquite, desert scrub, shinnery, tall grasses, and barbed-wire fences nearly covered with windblown sand. We turned onto a dirt road. Looking up at the top of a grove of trees, I noticed a great horned owl roosting on a limb. My hopes were

that it had not devoured the hawk during the night. When we finally stopped at a gate at the end of yet another dirt road, we were surrounded by the stillness of nature.

Having parked in this same spot the day before, the men felt we had a chance of finding the hawk. "It wouldn't fly, and we thought it might be hungry. So we left it some doves right here," said one of the hunters as he pointed to an area near the truck. Deciding to split up, I chose to walk north while the guys headed south.

Not ten feet from the truck, I spotted an array of feathers from a dove. Hoping that the hawk had carried the food in this direction, I slowly and as quietly as possible continued to follow a trail of feathers. Since I was close to the fence line, I had to watch my every step because, in places, the sand was ankle-deep or more. Not wanting to alarm the bird if it was ahead, I tried not to disturb rocks or step on dead twigs from surroundings bushes. Ahead was an impasse of dense brush and deep sand. To go around it would take too much time. I saw more feathers. Surely that hawk couldn't be very far away.

Deciding to continue between the

fence and the scrub, I was up to my right knee in sand. Dirt was sifting into my shoes. On my left was a large enough creosote bush to grab for balance. As I stayed upright, I peered down through the scraggly plant and saw the bird. It wasn't a hawk.

Looking up at the sky and trying to catch my breath, I glanced down at the bird again. The hooked bill, both toothed and notched, the dark "mustache" extending down the pale feathers of the neck, the taloned feet, the streaked chest indicated to me it was a first-year, juvenile peregrine falcon. The moment was mine to savor for the rest of my life.

Not taking my eyes off the bird, I called to the men to bring the net. I had found their bird. "Walk, don't run," I cautioned as they neared the area. With the falcon unable to fly, we would be able to snare the bird even if it left the protection of the bush. Instead, it pressed itself against the earth. With the net over it, I felt as if I could breathe again.

"Do you realize what you have found?" I asked the men. From my excitement, they knew something was unusual.

Never did I think I would ever rescue a bird that was endangered. Art and I had seen peregrines migrate through this area on several occasions. A road leading from Interstate-20 to the Andrews highway seemed to be a beacon for the falcons in early October. For some reason, this falcon was a month early.

Examining the bird, I could tell that the falcon had broken one of its wings at the wrist. At the speed these birds fly, it could easily have clipped a power line or the branch of a tree. It had not been shot.

As we drove back to Big Spring, I thought of how this powerful falcon could dive at small to medium-sized birds and either catch them in flight or knock them to the ground. Its eyesight was amazing. Recognizing its prey 3,000 feet away, the bird could plunge toward it at 100-200 m.p.h. On its first migration, this falcon's unmatched speed would never be used again.

When we arrived at my house, I showed the hunters, Charlie Lewis and Cliff Talbot, pictures of the falcon and related how important their efforts at helping the bird had been. Then calls — to the South Plains Wildlife Rehabilitation Center in Lubbock and U.S. Fish & Wildlife, Department of the Interior — were placed.

At the center, Debbie Tennyson examined the peregrine falcon. Administering injections to prevent infection and swelling, she placed the bird in a carrier to rest. The outer part of the wing would require amputation. This male peregrine would be used as an educational bird and share a mew with the center's female peregrine named "Empress." Given the title of "Emperor," the falcon found on a desolate lease became one of the center's best ambassadors. For four years, his poise and stately presence graced educational presentations.

19. Barn Owl – "Firecracker"

Tyto alba

Walking through the storage yard of Sivalls Inc., the man headed toward the vessel that was to be shipped to Bakersfield, California, the next week. Fifteen feet tall, the four-foot-wide unit separated gas and liquids as a vital part of oil field equipment.

As he approached the vessel, he noticed the black plastic was gone from the flange area near the top. Ultraviolet rays and windy weather had shredded the protection. Since the unit would be refurbished before shipment, he wasn't too concerned about the interior. Detecting movement at the base of the structure, he quickly sidestepped. As he turned to make sure it wasn't a rattlesnake, the pipe wrench he was carrying struck the vessel. The clang didn't surprise him nearly as much as it did the three adult barn owls that flew out of the opening.

"Never have I seen anything so beautiful," he said during a phone call. "Two of the owls were typical in color; the other one was white." Not wanting anything to harm the owls, he added, "They were too pretty to let something happen."

Two of the owls headed south, while the third landed on a telephone pole at the end of the yard. Suspecting

there might be a nest inside, the man climbed to the opening and peered inside. Seven eggs lay on a thick layer of debris atop a metal plate. The odor of cast pellets, partially eaten mice and rats, plus waste, was ripe. To the owls it was home.

First, he contacted Odessa Animal Control. Referred to Texas Parks & Wildlife, he learned that with all of the game wardens out of the office, we were the next to call. After informing him of the length of incubation, and time in the nest before fledging, I told him I would be talking with a supervisor in Parks & Wildlife before any removal could occur.

Permission was granted to take the eggs to the South Plains Wildlife Rehabilitation Center in Lubbock. Construction deadlines could not be met if the owls were allowed the time needed to raise their young.

A cold front arrived during the early morning hours of June 24th, the day we were to collect the eggs. As we approached the vessel, I appreciated Art's telling me the opening would be about eleven feet above the ground and 14 inches in diameter. With a ladder in place and two men to hold it, we were almost ready. "Tap on the side of the vessel. I'd rather see any owls fly than to have to face them when I get up there," I said. The sound sent two owls, one of which was white, out of the opening.

We would have to work quickly due to the cold, thirty-mile-an-hour winds. The eggs had to be placed in a makeshift incubator before they cooled. The only problem was reaching the eggs that lay at the opposite side of the vessel. Not able to crawl through the opening, I asked if the men had a hoe or something for me to roll the eggs toward the opening. A welder produced a classic hoe, circa 1910. Using this vintage tool, I was able to get two to three eggs at a time across the floor. Climbing down the ladder, I handed them to Art, who hurried to the incubator in the car.

On the ride to Lubbock, we talked of how the mother owl had taken advantage of a unique nesting area. Once inside, she had a steel floor, protection from the elements, and a nice warm place for her eggs. From the amount of guano and debris, she probably had nested there for at least two years. After the eggs were placed in the center's incubator, we returned home.

Early on the morning of July 4th, the phone rang. An egg had hatched. Appropriately named "Firecracker," it was given to a volunteer who would raise it. E-mails and pictures of its progress would follow. The remaining eggs never hatched.

The demands of the newborn were incredible. The volunteer kept the owl with her constantly, whether at home or at the center. Its every need was met, including tidbits of mice. Soon pictures were arriving. From a downy handful and early feathering, from nestling to fledgling, we were thrilled to see the results of our rescue effort. After learning to kill its food and its success in the flight cage, Firecracker was released in late September.

Only later would we learn of Firecracker's effect on the volunteer. Some ten months before the owl hatched, the volunteer's daughter had died suddenly. Since the July holiday had always been a family time, the volunteer dreaded this particular 4th. When she had received the call to nurture the newborn, she said she couldn't. Distraught with grief, she couldn't imagine taking on such an arduous task. The manager of the center insisted. Finally, the volunteer agreed. The new arrival would prove to be notable for far more than the holiday.

The responsibility of 24-hour care for the bird was almost overwhelming. It was also consoling. As the days progressed, the volunteer came to understand that she would always mourn the death of her daughter. At the same time, she realized there was a tremendous need for her work at the center. From this episode with a tiny creature that needed her attention and skills evolved a volunteer who specializes in barn owls. Gail Barnes, assistant manager of the center, has often told us, "That bird saved my life."

20. Golden Eagle – "Thorn"

Aquila chrysaetos

The pickup wandered down the dirt roads as the man checked fence lines and headed toward tomorrow's work. Eighteen miles south of Stanton, the ranch offered an endless assortment of chores. Thanksgiving was only two days away. In his mind, the man was already anticipating the aromas coming from his wife's cooking.

Glancing across the tall grasses, he noticed the largest bird he had ever seen. After he stopped the truck, he watched to see if it would fly. Many minutes passed. The bird remained on the ground. Finally, the man thought about approaching the bird. Turning off the engine, he opened the door, stepped down, and eased to the front of the truck. Since he had been inside the vehicle, he guessed maybe it hadn't noticed him.

The bird turned in his direction. It did not fly. "Something's wrong," he thought, as he reached through the passenger window and grabbed his coat. Slowly he walked toward the large bird.

Close enough to try and capture it, the man knew what he would do if he were successful. Taking his jacket, he quickly covered the bird and carried it to the pickup.

With one arm around the bird, he used the other to lift the large Igloo beverage cooler from the truck bed. It was all he had. Lifting the lid, he placed the bird inside the cooler, removed the coat, and lowered the lid. Once the container was placed on the passenger seat, he dialed our number.

"It's either an eagle or the largest hawk I've ever seen," said Randy McCaleb. Since he had previously brought us a bird of prey, Randy knew to head toward Big Spring. His quick arrival told us he must have flown the distance.

As he walked toward our front porch with a large cooler, we couldn't believe Randy had put a bird in it. He said every two minutes or less, he had raised the lid so it would have enough oxygen. He also checked so often because he didn't want it to die.

Crouched inside and completely filling the container was a first-year golden eagle. Looking up at Randy, I gave him the news. "You have yourself an eagle!" Using the coat and wearing leather gloves, I anticipated the struggle and resistance of a healthy eagle as I transferred the bird from the cooler to our carrier. There was none.

Thanking Randy for bringing the eagle to us, we told him we would be in Lubbock at the wildlife rehabilitation center in less than two hours. He would be kept informed of its progress. When we notified the manager, she said the staff would be ready.

Discovered in the examination of the eagle were swollen feet and legs. Unable to obtain its food, the bird was weak and unable to fly. Closer observation of the bottom of the feet detected infection from porcupine quills and cactus thorns. Nature's defense for a mammal and a plant had caused the downfall of this eagle.

Everyone realized the eagle would have a lengthy recovery. They appropriately named the bird "Thorn." At first, a regimen of antibiotics and soaking of the feet several times a day provided improvement. For months, veterinarians would continue to remove quills, thorns, and dead tissue. The feet were bound to protect the healing process.

On Christmas Eve, Art and I had to make an unplanned trip to the center. While there, the manager asked me to help with Thorn. Holding the eagle while she unwrapped his feet, I was overwhelmed at the devotion of all the staff in the treatment of this bird.

As my hands held his legs and my arms pressed against his wings, I could readily appreciate the size and potential strength of an eagle. While waiting for the rebinding of its feet, I was instructed in how to administer therapy to the toes. During the drive home after dark, I told Art this was one Christmas Eve I'd never forget.

In the ensuing months, it was discovered that ligaments had been damaged. The eagle was unable to bend its toes. Prostheses, braces, and therapy were created to try to correct this problem. One week the eagle would rally. Then a sudden decline in its condition would occur. The manager consulted with numerous rehabilitation centers to ascertain if any procedure had been overlooked. She was repeatedly told, "You are doing what we would be doing, and more."

From the time of its arrival, Thorn had bonded with the manager. Daily she fed and medicated the bird. When the eagle seemed to give up, Debbie Tennyson stayed with him and even slept beside his cage or in his mew. Somehow, Thorn gained the will to continue.

In late summer, Debbie allowed Thorn to exercise in the flight cage. The eagle could fly the length of the facility, but his landings were hampered by his feet. In early September, I went with Debbie when she took Thorn outside to sit in the sun beside a pond located on the grounds of the center. She indicated there was a possibility that Thorn might not make it. Each time he was in a decline, it was harder to bring him back. The eagle had endured numerous painful treatments, and his will seemed to be failing. Having watched his suffering, successes, and endurance for ten months, I thoroughly understood her quandary.

On September 13, swelling feet and a refusal to eat signaled yet another decline. For Thorn, whose perseverance had touched us all, the decision for euthanasia was made. His spirit, his very essence, continues to encourage those who try to save wildlife.

21. Yellow-headed Blackbird

Xanthocephalus xanthocephalus

The drive from Fort Davis to Balmorhea had taken longer than usual. A strong cold front had drenched the area. The familiar twists and turns of the scenic drive had been masked and made extremely dangerous by rain, mist and fog. When we reached the plains, our visibility was still limited.

Almost to the intersection where our road met the highway that leads to Balmorhea and Pecos, the thick curtain of moisture parted. Ahead, gracing the top and middle strands of a barbed-wire fence, were sixty to seventy yellow-headed blackbirds. Their migration had been stalled by weather so soupy they could not fly.

The contrast between the males and females was notable. Smaller and browner, the females, with just a smidgen of yellow on their throats, were pretty much relegated to the middle wires. Dominating the top strands were the males with their bright yellow heads, necks, and upper breasts. The males' brilliant yellow and black decorated the fence for some distance. Of such events are vacations made.

A few days later as I was leaving work, the phone rang. "You have to come," pleaded an English professor

at our local Howard College campus. "It can't fly. You'll see it on the west side of the campus." Having changed into my "bird clothes," I could hardly believe that after having seen yellow-headed blackbirds on our trip, I would now have to attempt to rescue one.

Enjoying his stroll on the west lawn near a wooden fence, the male yellow-headed blackbird held his wings evenly. Although it is known these birds spend much of their time walking as they look for insects, this fellow paced the length of the fence, turned, and paced some more. Finally, he found an area with a low spot. Ducking his head, he disappeared.

As I walked around the end of the fence to see where he had gone, the bird saw me. Back under the fence he went. Running toward him, I had already figured out his next move, which was to go under the fence again. This would go on until one of us tired. The only way to stay up with the bird was to go over the fence after him. There was no other way I'd ever get him if I kept going to the end of the structure.

The wooden fence had horizontal members at the top and bottom of the slats. If I put my left foot on the side of the board, with hands on the top, and a slight jump, I could propel myself over the fence. It was similar to mounting a horse, only I would have to dismount quickly or the blackbird

would get too far ahead.

Figuring out that plan, the bird walked hurriedly toward the administration building. We played hide-and-seek in the landscape greenery. Then he headed toward the south fence. A car honked. Turning, I saw someone wave as once again I vaulted the fence. "Great," I thought. "They probably think I'm going out for the track team."

Losing count of how many times the blackbird went under the fence, I realized the chase had already taken 45 minutes. Every time I went over the fence, I would have sworn it was higher. Suddenly, this foot-long avian-wonder veered away from the fences and headed toward the inner campus. If he walked, I walked. When he scurried, so did I. Finally he turned into an area that offered a brick corner created by some architect's 45- degree angle. If I could keep him from getting past me, I'd have him. Cautiously approaching him, I tried to herd him closer into my trap.

During all this time, the blackbird had protested my presence with the most raucous noise imaginable. His clacking, squealing notes were anything but musical. Now as we faced each other, his tired, raspy voice was an indication that he had little energy to spare. Within two feet of him, I lunged and caught his tail. Screaming, he admonished me severely before I slipped

a towel over his head.

For several days after the chase, we heard from people who wondered what was going on at Howard College. It was amazing how many folks drive by the school during late afternoon.

Examining the yellow-headed blackbird, we discovered a hairline fracture in one of his wings. The muscle tone of an active bird had allowed him to hold his wings equally, but the break had grounded his activities and led to his capture. After his healing period at the wildlife center, the elegantly colored bird was released.

22. SWAINSON'S HAWK

Buteo swainsoni

Flying over the pond, the bird noticed movement on top of the dirt berm surrounding the surface. As it plunged toward the ground squirrel, the bird caught a talon in the plastic material sticking up above the edge. His primary feathers dipped into the surface. The drag on his wing caused the bird's feet and tail to strike the substance in the pond. Trying to stabilize his body while off-balance, the bird used his other wing in an attempt to rise from this peril. Unfortunately, the crude oil in an open pit had claimed a victim.

Struggling against the sticky product that now covered half of his wings, feet and tail, the large bird managed to pull himself from the edge of this black abyss. The weight of the thick oil hampered any attempt at flying. The bird started walking.

Driving to the drill site, an independent consultant for the oil company was making a final check for the day. West Texas crude had brought him from an area near Cody, Wyoming, to Andrews. Since the oil lease was near the road, the man glanced toward the reserve pit.

Between the road and the pit stood a hawk. At least half of its body was coated with oil.

The man stopped his truck, walked toward the bird, and picked it up. Taking it to his motel room, he called a veterinarian who told him to call us at once.

"Whatever you do, don't put that hawk in an enclosed area, such as a box. The fumes can be lethal to a bird," I warned. The man mentioned that he had wiped as much crude off the hawk as possible. Arrangements were made for him to deliver the hawk the next morning.

As we opened our front door, we were greeted by the removal of the man's western felt hat as he introduced himself. "David Ball," he said distinctly. "I'm pleased to meet you. I think the hawk may be a red-tail, but you can't tell 'cause his tail's so black." As we followed David to his pickup, I noticed the trail of dried caliche — a composite of calcium carbonate, gravel, sand and silt — that had fallen from his knee-high boots. Well-worn, they were an integral part of his daily uniform.

The truck must have sighed when it finally reached our driveway because clumps of dirt and caliche had fallen where it stopped. The man obviously worked in the oil fields. Inside, on the floor of the passenger side, was an oily black hawk standing on a piece of newspaper. It had ridden from Andrews to Big Spring in that position.

After identifying the hawk as a Swainson's, I picked it up and looked inside its mouth as it defensively opened its beak. The throat was clean, and only a trace of crude could be seen on the roof of the mouth. Since the oil had not penetrated through the feathers to the skin of its chest and abdomen, we felt the hawk had a chance to recover.

Thanking David for rescuing the hawk and bringing it to us, we cautioned him that we had a legal obligation to report this oiled bird to both federal and state officials. Well aware of the procedures, David said he would stop by the company's headquarters upon his return to Andrews. He would tell them he had brought the hawk to people who were licensed to care for wild birds, and that the Swainson's would be transported to Lubbock. "It's the right thing to do," he added.

At the South Plains Rehabilitation Center, the hawk was given the first of three baths. With a water temperature of 105 degrees and the blue detergent Dawn, the Swainson's feathers and feet went from black to partial coloration. The bottom of the basin was dark with the remnants of crude oil and dirt. The subsequent baths would remove more residues from its encounter with an open pit. Atropine, to counter any poisons, and charcoal for absorption were administered.

Two weeks later, the hawk was exercising in the flight cage. By late September, the Swainson's had returned to nature.

From that chance meeting with the man from Wyoming, we knew we encountered a remarkable person. While some try to dress a part, David Ball was the part. With his Stetson, neatly trimmed handlebar mustache, crisp shirt and jeans, tall boots, and articulate renditions of his own success in helping birds of prey, we believed his colorful outward appearance matched his inner integrity.

23. American Bittern

Botaurus lentiginosus

A family visit had brought the young man to Waterloo, Iowa. While on a college campus, he was approached by three different people who knew he lived in Odessa. "Are you taking that bird to Texas?" each inquired. "What bird?" was his reply. "The one in the paper and on the radio," they answered.

Knowing nothing of the media blitz to try and obtain a bird's safe passage to South Plains Wildlife Rehabilitation Center in Lubbock, Alex Carstens checked the local newspaper. After he placed a call, he drove to the Black Hawk Wildlife Rehabilitation Project to pick up his passenger. He was well aware that vehicle transport was fine as long as the trip was accomplished in one day.

Greeted by Terese Evans, Alex learned that the American bittern had been found near a pet store under some shrubbery. With a bruised and broken wing, the bird had spent a month recovering from its injury. The last of October was too late for the bittern to be released. Its own kind had already migrated. Questionable was whether the bird could even make such an arduous journey. Needing to have the secretive water bird trans-

ported to a southern state for release, and not knowing any "snow birds" that might assist this "bird," the president of the Black Hawk Project managed to get the word out to the public.

With approval from U. S. Fish & Wildlife for the bittern to be carried across state lines to another licensed wildlife center, Terese was delighted to meet Alex. With snow predicted for Iowa the following week, the bittern needed a warmer climate immediately.

After Alex left with his passenger, Terese alerted the South Plains center that the bird was on its way. Included in this conversation was the young man's parting comments. He said he felt that part of our job here on earth was to be stewards of the land and the animals, and this was such an easy thing for him to do. He thanked her for allowing him to take the bittern.

The director of South Plains called to advise us that the young man and his avian cargo were leaving Waterloo. Driving through Kansas City, Missouri, to the Fort Worth area, Alex would continue on Interstate-20 to Big Spring. We were to meet him and bring the bittern to Lubbock. Expecting him the next day, we were given his cell number, which we called.

Alex wanted to check in every two hours to give us his location. We were concerned about his driving all night with no relief. Close to midnight he called to say he was going to pull off the road and sleep a few hours. He would check back in around 7:00 a.m. When the phone rang shortly after six the next morning, we couldn't have been happier. Alex had slept for two hours, then continued down the road.

When he was to check in again, the phone was silent. More than an hour went by and no Alex. Finally, he called. A flat had delayed him. He and the bird were fine.

As morning turned into early afternoon, Alex notified us as to his expected arrival at the truck stop north of town. He was right on time. After having talked with him many times during the last 24 hours, we were delighted to meet the young man who cared so much for wildlife. Spending too short a time with him, we realized he was very tired and needed to go on to Odessa and a long sleep.

Since we had another bird coming in that afternoon, we drove to Lamesa and delivered the bittern to Julie Boatright, who had served as an intern at the wildlife center. She helped com-

plete the bird's journey to Lubbock.

Driving back to Big Spring, we talked about how sometimes it takes so many people to assure a bird's success and return to the wild, and that included an Alex Carstens. He was an exceptional young man. Not believing in mere chance or circumstances, Alex definitely felt he was meant to bring the bittern 1,125 miles to us.

24. Barn Owl

Tyto alba

A COLD AND DUSTY NORTHEAST WIND stung the farmer's face as he stepped down from his pickup. Walking to the concrete pad that supported an empty tank, he knelt to examine the perimeter of the vessel. As the man inched along the metal sides, he noticed a long, narrow opening that rust and neglect had created. Glancing inside, he was surprised to see a large bird lying on the floor.

"Five by fifteen," was the reply the farmer gave when he told me of his water tank with a bird trapped inside. Envisioning a typical galvanized steel stock tank, I assumed he meant

**ONLY WHEN I
PUT MY HANDS
ON HIS WINGS
AND PLACED HIM
IN A THICK BAG
DID THE OWL
AROUSE ENOUGH
TO EXTEND HIS
TALONS IN
DEFIANCE...**

five feet tall and fifteen feet in diameter. "No, ma'am. It's fifteen feet tall and five feet wide."

Since the man only had a six-foot ladder, we would need to carry ours with us. Only three feet shy of the top of the tank, we figured we could use an old blanket to fashion a saddle on the rim of the vessel. Standing on top of the ladder, Art could then swing a leg over the rim and sit astride the blanket. I would follow. Then Art would lift the ladder over the top and lower it inside the tank. While he remained at the top, he could help me get down to the top of the ladder. Once at the bottom of the tank, I could capture the bird.

Traveling north, then east of Coahoma, we met the farmer and followed him to the abandoned tank in the midst of plowed barren fields. Earlier, the farmer had mentioned he thought the bird was an owl, but he wasn't sure what type. When we reached the top of the tank, we could see that it was a barn owl.

There was no movement of the bird in spite of our noise in handling and climbing the ladder. Only when I put my hands on his wings and placed him in a thick bag did the owl arouse enough to extend his talons in defiance. With no way to see anything through the material of his enclosure, the barn owl grew quiet and still.

Relieved that the bird was out of the tank, we talked with the farmer about how the owl managed to get to the bottom of the vessel. Having rescued owls from chimneys and attics, I told him birds can half-fly and hop across short distances. We felt the barn owl had zig-zagged its way down the sides of the tank by jumping from side to side. The rough, rusty texture of the decaying structure had offered footholds sufficient for the owl's descent.

Once on the bottom, the owl may have captured mice that could enter through small holes near the floor. Without food coming in, the bird had begun to suffer the effects of starvation. It did not have the strength to get back out of the tank.

After a tube feeding, the barn owl was taken to a wildlife center for extended care. After being able to tolerate a solid diet, it started short flights in an outdoor exercise cage. From a lonely brush with death, the raptor now had a chance for recovery and release.

25. Eared Grebe

Podiceps nigricollis

Instinctively, the small water bird searched for a place to land. Tired from flying through a December storm during the night, it saw ahead the wet, glistening surface it sought. Regardless of the tall, round structures adjacent to the water, the bird had to set down to rest.

Instead of sinking into the supposed pond, and floating at ease through the rest of the night, the little bird felt the sudden impact of asphalt on its feet and legs. Even with its wings beating to slow it, the bird skidded a few yards, then stopped. Unable to walk, it wiggled clumsily into a darkened area to await the dawn.

"Who'd a thought we'd have thunder and lightning at this time of the year?" joked the unit foreman with some of the yard crew. Leaving the warmth of the control room, he indicated he'd be back as soon as he checked an area affected by the storm.

As the foreman walked through the refinery, he occasionally waved at other men on duty. Having weathered another storm without major outages, he turned to start his walk back, but stopped when he detected a movement on the ground under one of the large vessels. With his flashlight, he discovered a small visitor.

Struggling against the large, rough hands that suddenly grabbed it, the water bird was no match for the foreman. After he placed it inside his coat, the bird was still. When he entered the control room, he bellowed, "You guys aren't going to believe what I found!"

Fortunately, there was little debris on the concrete pad under the vessel. The bird appeared to be clean. Taking some rags from the bin, the men made a thick nest in a cardboard box for the delicate creature that had arrived with the storm. Knowing it wasn't a duck, they wondered just what it could be.

During breakfast, the phone rang. From the description given by a plant employee, we felt we knew what specie had been found. When we arrived at the refinery we were able to identify it as an eared grebe. Its winter plumage was nondescript. Gone were the golden tufts or plumes which accent the head behind the bird's scarlet eyes during breeding season. Even the black on the head, neck, and back seemed to have faded. Its slender, short pointed bill and lobed feet were the telltale signs of identification. Essentially, the water bird was black above, white to grey below. Only a whitish patch back of its ears dignified its drab appearance. Nature had certainly helped the grebe to blend with the starkness of winter.

For a bird that feeds, sleeps, courts, and even has a floating nest on water, the eared grebe had been desperate as it searched for a place to land. A diving, swimming bird, the grebe, except in flight, spends its life on water. Depending upon where it summered, the little bird was heading either to an inland, freshwater lake, our saline lakes, or the seacoast. Its inland diet would include small fish, insects and their lar-

FOR A BIRD THAT FEEDS, SLEEPS, COURTS, AND EVEN HAS A FLOATING NEST ON WATER, THE EARED GREBE HAD BEEN DESPERATE AS IT SEARCHED FOR A PLACE TO LAND.

vae. The Gulf would provide crustaceans as well.

Since the grebes are known to be weak fliers, this bird may have been "puddle hopping." Resembling a small duck while in flight, the grebe would have used any body of water on its way south. Its unfortunate detour could have meant disaster. Unable to become airborne unless it had a running start on the water's surface, the little bird would have had a slim chance of survival if it had not been found.

A bathtub check of the grebe's ability to use its feet and legs was a pleasure, both to us and the bird. Enjoying the deep water, it dove to the bottom of the tub and swam the length underwater.

It was well prepared to dive swiftly and swim rapidly when threatened. With hardly any tail, the grebe was equipped with legs located at the rear of its body. In flight, the bird's feet would be extended behind to help steer it.

On an area pond with sufficient length for the grebe's departure, we said goodbye to the winter visitor. Even as sleet pelted us, the eared wonder welcomed another "puddle" on his way to freedom.

RESEMBLING A SMALL DUCK WHILE IN FLIGHT, THE GREBE WOULD HAVE USED ANY BODY OF WATER ON ITS WAY SOUTH. ITS UNFORTUNATE DETOUR COULD HAVE MEANT DISASTER.

26. RING-NECKED PHEASANT

Phasianus colchicus

The first sunshine in over a week brought a bright, morning light into our home. Accustomed to early rising, I welcomed the glare on the bedroom windows. The severity of the winter storm, that barged into town on Christmas Eve and continued for days, had left a glistening but dangerous landscape. The overture of sleet had warned us of what was to come. Followed by six to eight inches of snow, the weather had spanned the holidays and welcomed the new year.

During the afternoon, our enjoyment of the fireplace was interrupted by the telephone: "On the north side of the retirement center building, there's a large bird huddled in the snow. We can't tell what it is. It's just a big bundle of feathers." Art and I donned boots, coveralls, down coats, hats and gloves. If the bird couldn't fly and decided to lead us on a chase across the center's vast lawn, we might be outside for a while. A net on a long pole and a 30-foot roll of netting might equalize the bird's attempt at an escape.

Not even knowing if the "bundle" was injured, could fly or run, we drove and slid the four blocks to reach our destination. Fortunately, we lived on the same street, so our arrival was fairly quick.

From the street, we could see the brownish lump against the side of the building. To reach it would require a walk across part of the lawn. The crunching of ice and snow might waken and alarm the bird.

Street noise, for once, was welcome. As people decided to chance a drive during this break in the weather, it would hopefully mask our approach.

Only a few steps away from the bird, we silently motioned to each other that this was the moment to use the pole net. Art signaled his usual "use it quickly" advice. With perhaps only one chance for success, I placed the net over the bronze and brown-red feathers flecked with black, brown, and white.

Not only did the bird awake, it exploded upward. Holding the net against the snowy ground, I realized we had just captured a male ring-necked pheasant.

A bird of the Great Plains and northern Texas Panhandle, the pheasant might have been one of many previously introduced into our own Howard County. The effort to establish the birds for hunting had failed due to lack of food and cover. Of more concern, however, was the condition of the pheasant. It had been scalped.

As it struggled against the netting, Art carefully removed the large bird and placed it in a carrier. Having fallen to my knees as the net slipped over the pheasant, I was grateful to him for helping me up and brushing snow from my lower legs.

Once home, we were still astonished at the bird's condition. All flesh and feathers from the top of the head were gone. The exposed skull was dry and surrounded by skin that tightly adhered to the head. Fortunately, the pheasant's circulatory system in that area had suffered spasms that closed the flow of blood in the vessels. It kept the bird from dying.

The "bundle" everyone had seen was the bird taking one of its wings to cover its head as it slept. The ring-neck had been successful in keeping the top of its head warm during the severe cold.

When the caller had described the bird as large, she was correct. Almost three feet long, the pheasant's wingspan was nearly 32 inches. At over two and a half pounds, it let you know its presence, especially with its

clawed feet that are used to scratch the ground for food. Typical coloration for a male was its white collar, iridescent green-blue to purple head and neck, and the noticeable patch of red skin on the cheeks. The long, pointed tail feathers, stout bill, and long legs lent to his regal appearance.

Introduced into the United States in the mid- to late 1800s, the ring-necked pheasant thrives on open farmlands that offer corn, wheat, oats, barley, and hay. Tall grasses and weeds provide extra food and convenient hiding places. From the strength of this bird, we could imagine how quickly it would flush and leave hunters dismayed.

No other injuries were evident. One guess was that a winter hawk had attacked the bird. Its head would be one of the first targets to peck once it was under control. With its strength the pheasant might have wiggled free of the predator and flown for its life.

Taking the ring-neck to a wildlife center, we couldn't help but laugh when a volunteer suggested making a toupee for the hatless bird. If the proper adhesive was available and a veterinarian approved, a "patch" would be added to the bird's coloration and it could sport a year-round addition to its wardrobe.

27. Barn Owl

Tyto alba

Before dawn, the wind against the windows confirmed the weather forecast. Promised in the early morning hours, the southwesterly gusts encouraged the weather stripping to sing. Since it was impossible to sleep with the incessant howling, the man decided to get an early start on the long day.

As the pickup headed into the wind, he checked the ranch's fence line for any breaks. Almost to the gate after some fifteen miles, the man noticed in the distance something caught and flapping on the top strand of the barbed wire. "Another plastic bag," he thought.

Although employed to accomplish many of the jobs required by a working ranch, the man took a personal pride in the land that had sustained him and his wife for years. Daily he saw the effects of paper, plastics, and cans carelessly discarded along the roadway.

Approaching the fluttering object, he realized that what was caught on the wire was the wing of a barn owl. Fortunately, the raptor's feet were supported by another strand of wire and coyote fencing. Otherwise, it would have had all of its weight on the captured wing.

In a hurry to free the owl from the wire, he never even thought of the leather gloves on the seat beside him. Quietly closing the truck's door, he walked toward the struggling and frightened bird. Without another thought, he grabbed the predator barehanded. As he pressed the owl against his chest, he freed the bird from the barbs and carefully folded the injured wing toward the body. At that moment, having wiggled enough to free a leg, the bird sank four talons into the man's hand.

"What did you do then?" I asked, as the owl's rescuer described his latest bird adventure. Having already brought us a golden eagle, he was capable of many challenges. He replied that choices had to be made. If he let go of the bird, he might not be able to catch it again. Since he knew it was injured, he felt he must hold on to the owl and somehow free his hand from the painful grip.

Sitting down, he held the owl in his lap. Three of the talons were in the palm of his hand. Slowly he pried each sharp hooked claw out of his flesh. While keeping the bird from using those talons, he pulled the last long, sharp nail from the back of his hand.

With the barn owl's legs under control, the man extended the injured wing for a closer look. Upon delivering the bird to us, he commented that he thought no bones were broken.

Later that day, I called him to confirm that miraculously no bones were affected. While one barb had cut a thin line in the skin on the underside of the wing, the other barbs had only inflicted small punctures. Because the owl had been found early during such an ordeal, we felt it had been spared damage that would warrant amputation or euthanasia.

During our conversation, I told the man that when releasing barn owls, seeing their silent flight over open country was our reward. A gift of nature had equipped them with soft-edged feathers that reduced any sound emitted by the flow of air over their wings.

Through the years we have come to appreciate not only their eyesight, but also their ability to locate their prey by hearing. When their eyes might be deceived by the darkest of nights, the owls could still detect the slightest movement of their next meal.

As we closed our chat, I asked the man about his hand. "It'll be fine in a few days," was his answer. Having had the same experience, I knew that the harder you try to remove a raptor's talons, the tighter it will grip. In spite of the excruciating pain, the man had put the owl's survival as his first priority.

The next day we delivered the barn owl to the wildlife center in Lubbock. Administering antibiotics and anti-inflammatory medications, Gail Barnes confirmed that the bird had no broken bones and would probably be releasable. Twenty-two days later, we shared the good news of the owl's release with the man who had found it hanging on a fence "in the middle of nowhere."

28. American Robin

Turdus migratorius

ALTHOUGH IT HAD RAINED THE DAY before, the neighbor turned on her sprinklers, creating a sparkling mist in the early morning light. Patiently waiting in the massive mulberry trees was a flock of birds. As the sprinkler heads receded into the lush grass, the songbirds descended en masse in their hunt for food.

Each bird practiced the same behavior — a quick-paced walk, almost a run of several feet. Stopping, they would look from side to side, and listen. Then their antics were repeated. Suddenly, one would plunge its yellow beak

A ROBIN SLUMPED
ON THE GRASS.
THE WOMAN'S
SCREAM AND THE
BURST OF THE
BOY'S BB GUN
CAUSED THE FLOCK
OF SONGBIRDS
TO EXPLODE
IN FLIGHT.

through the grass and into the soil. Extracting a wiggling earthworm, the bird readily swallowed the morsel in one extended gulp. With such success, the others sensed they, too, would find something to eat.

The hungry members of the flock soon spilled over into adjacent yards. The previous day's rain had softened the earth, and numerous worms were readily found. Satisfied, the flock soon reunited in a live oak to preen.

Having watched the return and feeding frenzy of her favorite springtime birds, the homeowner left her kitchen window to start her daily routine. There would be other times during the day when she could watch them.

That afternoon, the woman heard the school bus stopping at the corner. Neighborhood children — with books, backpacks and no-longer-needed jackets — walked in several directions on their way home. As one of the students passed her yard, she noticed he was looking into the trees. He probably saw all those birds this morning, she thought.

Entering his home, the youngster immediately went to his room. His most treasured gift from Christmas was waiting on him. Having fixed him an after-school snack, his mother told him she would be home as soon as she met his dad at the airport. She reminded him to start on his homework.

Much later and tired of studying, the boy could see through his bedroom shutters that those birds were now in the neighbor's yard. Hurrying outside, he was careful not to scare them away. Intent upon finding worms or insects, the flock was not unduly disturbed by his presence. Sidling to another part of the yard, they seemed tolerant of the boy's measured approach.

Once again enjoying her view of the feeding birds, the woman saw her neighbor's son. Running out the front door, she yelled as he pulled the trigger. A robin slumped on the grass. The woman's scream and the burst of the boy's BB gun caused the flock of songbirds to explode in flight.

Horrified and angry, the woman crossed her yard and approached the boy. At that moment, his parents pulled into the driveway. Having seen their son aim and fire the rifle was a sickening disappointment. The Christmas gift had been given only after much discussion with their son before and after the holidays.

As they left their car, their neighbor signaled for the parents to stop. The adults noticed that the rifle now lay discarded in the wet grass. About a foot from the bird, the boy with head down wasn't moving. Noticing the tears running down his cheeks, the threesome waited for the boy to experience the impact of what he had done.

"It's not dead," said a frantic voice on the phone. "His parents took him inside while I picked it up. Planned on burying it, but it wasn't limp," the woman added. Having put the bird on some towels in a cardboard box, she had seen that it was breathing. "Can I bring it to you?"

When we opened the box, the robin appeared to be asleep. The lady's placing it in a quiet, dark place allowed the bird some recovery time from the shock and stress of being shot. We both could see that the left eye was grazed by the small pellet.

Its dark brick-red chest indicated the bird was a male robin. The female's breast would be a duller, paler coloration. Both sexes would have the almost black head, wings, and tail. The greyish feathers on top, long legs, and white around the eye completed the distinguishing marks of the spring visitor.

Walking the lady back to her car, I told her the robin had a chance. Not only was a wildlife sanctuary available, but also a veterinarian who had helped us with our cat. When a cactus thorn had become imbedded in the middle of his eyeball, I had watched as the vet extracted the object. I felt confident the robin would have the best care possible.

The woman left with the assurance that the bird would be held at the wildlife center for whatever time was necessary. For it to be capable of returning to nature was important. Several hours later I called the bird's rescuer. "Robin redbreast" was awake and active.

"IT'S NOT DEAD,"
SAID A FRANTIC
VOICE ON
THE PHONE.
"HIS PARENTS
TOOK HIM
INSIDE WHILE
I PICKED IT UP...

73

29. Great Horned Owl

Bubo virginianus

The night provided a hunting bonanza for the large bird. Clutched in its talons, a cottontail rabbit was one of several that had scampered across its vision. As the raptor finished tearing the remaining flesh from the carcass, the mesquite, in which it was perched, shook. Suddenly the ground beside it erupted.

Instinctively, the bird of prey tightly gripped the limb and hunkered down while the sudden rain covered its head, back, and wings. Trying to fling the moisture from its feathers, the bird struggled with the burning sensation in one eye. Accustomed to weathering downpours, the raptor endured the brief but heavy deluge.

In the control room at the refinery, the worker had just poured himself another cup of coffee. Glancing back at the monitor, the man noticed a pressure loss. Reacting immediately to what would become a major problem, he spilled the hot liquid onto his lap as he immediately started the procedures in handling the ruptured pipeline.

After a severe December and early January, the weather had seemed almost spring-like, even into the first three weeks of February. What was usually a slower time of the year for

bird rescue ended with a phone call: "There's a black owl out here, and it won't fly," said the lady. Since she had seen the bird hanging around her property for several days, she decided something could be wrong. Knowing there is no such owl, I was very curious about what she had seen.

Nestled among the native junipers, the woman's home was secluded from the road. Offering privacy and a natural beauty, the surrounding terrain was hilly, rocky, and filled with even more junipers, grasses, cactus, and a few scraggly mesquites. A cleared area between the house and greenery allowed for a yard. At the end of this lawn, where the juniper dominated, stood what appeared to be two gold eyes looking out from the top of a large, black cookie jar.

With one "horn," or tuft of feathers, plastered to its head and the other standing straight up, a great horned owl glared back at us. As I netted the raptor, I was troubled by its condition. Coated with crude oil and grit, its wings, tail, head, and chest looked as if it were wearing a big, black coat. Remarkably, my leather gloves had very little residue from the bird. The coating had hardened and encapsulated

the feathers.

After placing the owl in a carrier, I asked the lady if there had been an oil spill. Taking me to another part of her property, she showed me an area where, in January, earth-moving equipment had moved junipers and covered the rock with dirt. As I walked deeper into the dense growth, I could see the effects of the spill had traveled much further.

Assured that I would let her know the outcome, the lady waved as the owl and I headed back to town. Once home, after failing to reach the game warden, I contacted the sheriff's department for assistance in locating him. Since a spill was probably common knowledge, I called my friend at the Herald. He knew nothing of any oil spills, but would start checking.

On his way to the spill site, the game warden called and said he would be back in touch. Later that day, he notified us that the spill, traveling downhill, had gone 1 ½ -miles from Silver Heels to the edge of the municipal golf course. Without the ability to shut down the pipeline, the spill theoretically could have coursed through the golfing area and city park to Comanche Lake. By closing valves

Thin from existing a month on the ground, from the time of the rupture until its rescue, the great horned owl had no evidence of oil in its mouth. Somehow it had managed to catch animals that had not been affected by the spill. Miraculously, the owl had no oil on its skin, thanks to its dense feathers. If it had, the oil would have been absorbed by its body and damaged internal organs. Once at my home, it readily ate freshly thawed mice and looked for more.

Chemicals in the crude had affected the bird's eyes. The pupil of one eye was a pinpoint, while the other was wide open. Having handled other raptors with the same problem, I had seen some recover with time. With the healing of the eye and removal of the caked mess on its feathers, the great horned owl would be considered for release.

Grateful for the survival of our walking evidence, we recognized the strength of its perseverance. From a night like no other, the dingy, comical-looking owl had alerted us that our and its environment had been threatened.

and relieving the pressure moving the crude through the pipe, the operator had prevented a serious event from becoming an even larger environmental problem.

The contractor, hired by the pipeline company, had tried to cover up rather than remove the effects of the rupture. The game warden verified the extent of the damage. Since a federally and state protected specie had suffered the consequences of the failure of the line, an agreement was reached that the length of the spill would be cleaned.

30. GOLDEN EAGLE

Aquila chrysaetos

In the early morning fog, driving was slow and tedious. Usually, her drive to work was the best part of the day. Hawks were readily seen perched in the bare mesquites, on fence posts, and a particular telephone pole that was the high point between her house and Midland.

With her windshield wipers clearing the persistent moisture, she looked forward to seeing what would be on the pole that morning. As the seasons changed, so did the pole's occupants. A safe place to rest during the night, the structure offered a tremendous view of the surrounding open country. Any mammal noted by a bird of prey's keen eyesight could easily be captured for a meal.

As the road dipped for a natural drainage area, the fog slowed her progress to a crawl. Coming out of the dense barrier, the swipe of the wiper revealed a large, dark bird atop the pole. "My God, that's an eagle," she thought. "Couldn't be anything else, it's so big." She stopped in the roadway.

Uneasy and wary of the large object that was only a few fence posts away, the raptor crouched. Using its feet and legs to spring into the air, the eagle, with its quick wing beats,

rapidly left the area and disappeared into the fog.

For several mornings afterwards, the woman continued to look for the eagle. Only the usual red-tailed hawks graced the top of the pole. She guessed that was her one and only chance to see an eagle in the wild.

As February turned into March, the lady's drive became routine again. The wintering hawks seemed to have left, and it would be a while before the summer raptors returned. In the low area south of the telephone pole she noticed a big bird on the ground about thirty feet inside the fence line. Dark brown, it was the size of the eagle she had previously seen. Pulling over into the grass beside the road, she stopped the car. "It has to be my eagle."

This time the raptor didn't leap into flight and leave. Instead, it ran a few feet, stopped, and jumped. Struggling to become airborne, the eagle was unable to control its long, round wings. Awkwardly, it set back down in the grass. Although its primary feathers kept touching the earth, the bird made several more attempts at flying.

Realizing that something was wrong with the eagle, she called us as soon as she reached her office. With the exact location of the bird, I called Parks & Wildlife. Upon arriving at the site, a game warden could find no bird. His office had been receiving calls for several days about a large

brown bird somewhere along the county road. This was the first exact location he had been given. Alerting the lady that the warden would continue checking the area, I asked that she maintain her daily vigil.

In response to yet another call, the warden checked the area again. Using his binoculars, he scanned 180 degrees of scrubby brush, cactus, and mesquites. Beside an agarita bush loaded with potential blooms, he found the bird. "Need some help out here," he told his captain. "There really is a bird. It's a golden eagle," he said with relief. "I'm staying with it. We'll need Animal Control to help."

"How did you finally capture it?" was my first question when the warden called. Saying it wasn't easy, he added, "That sucker had a bunch of grown men running like crazy. Guess it finally wore out. They put a net over it when it bumped into a telephone pole. Otherwise, it would have crossed the road and gone into the brush again."

Once at our home, we examined the eagle's wings. Extended, they had a span of six and a half feet. One had no evidence of a break. The other wing had the telltale lump or calcification of a healing fracture. Otherwise, the raptor was healthy.

As the eagle dined on mice, we were able to see the golden hackles on the back of its neck and head. The rest

of the feathers were a dark brown, as were its eyes. Its black bill and talons were convincing evidence of a large, powerful bird. Although smaller than a female, this male had managed to subsist on rabbits, ground squirrels, rats, and birds while trying to survive.

Handing the "golden" over to the manager of the wildlife center in Lubbock, we learned that the calcification was probably two to three weeks old. That was about the time frame given by the numerous sightings of the eagle on the ground.

Although it was determined that the golden eagle would never be able to soar again, or dive toward its prey at 150-200 miles an hour, the raptor was taken to west-central New Mexico. Upon entering the Zuni Indian reservation, the eagle, as all eagles before him, was blessed by their medicine man. Following this private ceremony, the bird was taken to their sanctuary for golden and bald eagles. Placed with other non-releasable goldens, it would be allowed to live out its life. Overseen by a veterinarian employed by the Albuquerque Zoo, the huge facility was truly "eagle heaven" for an earthbound bird.

31. Great Horned Owl

Bubo virginianus

"We have a problem," came unexpectedly from a city employee, Shirley Cross. "Two baby owls in a tank at the water treatment plant." She explained that the nest was about fifteen to twenty feet down on the inside wall of the grinder vessel. Since the city planned to clean, repair and reuse the facility, the process would disturb the owl family. When I told her we would go out and look at the situation, she added, "It's a heck of a place to have young."

One of the plant workers took us to the east side of the large tank. He said the owls were on the other side of the wall, inside the tank, in a manhole. It was then we realized that what we saw above the ground was only part of the vessel. Below the manhole, the structure extended downward perhaps another eight feet. The top of the tank had been removed and was lying in the grass to the north.

Climbing the steel stairway to the top of the concrete structure, we saw the manhole across the tank on the east side. Inside were two great horned owl nestlings. Covered with down and emerging feathers, they stood at the opening and looked out at their environment. No trees or grasses to stimulate their vision. No birds taking flight or insects to tempt their curiosity; instead, an empty sky and gray, caked matter below.

Our guide pointed out that the gray matter on the floor of the structure was sludge. Some five to six feet deep, the dried waste was about three feet below the nest. It would not be threatening to the nestlings unless it rained, he thought. If the young owls, after leaving the nest and not ready for flight, were to land in puddles caused by a downpour, the birds would be standing in toxic material. Methane gas was also of concern. We informed him that since young fledglings are nearly ten to twelve weeks old before they start to fly, the twosome might be on the dangerous surface for weeks.

"Shirley, we need a crane. Please call Cathey," was my request after realizing the inaccessibility of the nest. Thinking it would take a day or two to get the equipment, we were surprised by her return call, "How about this afternoon?"

The crane was at the plant when we arrived. Jack Cathey and crew were preparing the steel cage and cables. While we waited, one of the city's employees said he frequently saw one of the parents roosting nearby. With the abundant mice and rabbit population, he felt that the mother owl was finding plenty of food for her young. The sound of the crane's engine signaled an end to our conversation.

Approaching the cage, another of the plant's employees said he would get the birds. "No, I'll be handling the owls," was my answer. Assuring him that he was certainly capable of grabbing the birds, I added that we were now responsible. His offer was appreciated. However, in capturing the nestlings, if he inadvertently injured one, I would be held accountable and my license would be in jeopardy.

As the cage began its smooth ascent, Art and I remembered another ride provided by Cathey Construction. When birds of prey located their nests in almost impossible sites, it often required the expertise of a crane crew to get us there. This was no exception.

On board with us was Jack Cathey, who was constantly communicating with his operator in the crane's cab. After rising above the thick, concrete wall of the vessel, we slowly descended inside toward the opening and the owls. Keeping the cage from contacting the wall was essential. If frightened, one of the nestlings might fall or jump from the nest to the sludge below.

While Jack talked with his crewman, Art kept a hand ready so that the cage could not touch the wall. Finally, we were in front of the opening. The siblings had a typical reaction. Instead of coming towards danger and us, they remained at the back of the nest.

As Art opened the cage's gate, the nestlings snapped their bills, slightly spread their wings, and tried to threaten us away. Instinctively, they were trying to look larger and meaner than they were. "Keep me close," I cautioned, as I put one foot on the manhole pipe, and leaned in to reach for the first owl. Not knowing what I would do, the fluffy creatures actually looked surprised to have something suddenly gripping their legs. As I turned toward Art with the second one, I glanced upward. Todd Darden, director of Public Works, was watching from the top of the vessel. He, Shirley, Jack and the men who had found the owls had been instrumental in making this intervention successful.

Before leaving the nest site, we looked at the makeshift home. A thin layer of twigs, down from the mother, bones, rabbit fur, feathers, and the remains of small birds, lined the modest abode. Crumbled among the debris were the remains of pellets cast by the parent owls and nestlings. This thin layer of bedding separated the young from the surface of the pipe. The "aroma" of excrement that had not made it over the side of the nest, and decaying animal matter produced the familiar aroma of an owl's nest.

Although none of us humans, that April day, had been privy to the noisy hooting and bowing of the courtship of their parents, we were thrilled with the retrieval of these buff-colored offspring. Knowing that they would grow into the largest, most powerful of American owls was satisfaction at its utmost.

32. Barn Owls

Tyto alba

Maneuvering through the opening that was designed to accommodate the tail of a B-29, the bird of prey used the entrance nightly to access the Commemorative Air Force (CAF) hangar. Ghosts of the past dotted the vast floor of this tribute to World War II flight abilities. As she had done previously, the night flier circled before landing. Located on a preferred spot on the horizontal steel beams that lined the sides of the building were six eggs she was incubating.

Distracted by a sudden noise, she misjudged her approach. After the upper part of her wing slammed into one of the planes, she fell to the floor. The barn owl was grounded.

Called to pick up the owl, Harry Hopkins, a Midland volunteer, was upset when he later described the bird's condition. "The wing's a mess." When he delivered the bird, we could readily see the damage and the hopelessness of the situation. "Do you think there's a nest in that building?" we asked. Our question was answered the next day.

Phoning from the hangar, Mark Baxter, a CAF mechanic, inquired about the owl. After being told that the injury was so severe euthanasia was required, he said he would check to see if the female had chosen the hangar as a nest site. After some time, the phone rang. "Six white eggs on the beam above the north door. One is starting to hatch. Do you think the mate can raise them by himself?" asked Mark.

Of equal importance was whether the male would abandon the nest. Since both sexes assist in incubation, and pairs were often found sitting side by side, with a portion of eggs under each parent, this was a situation that would require constant monitoring. Laid at different intervals, the eggs would hatch in sequence and the young would vary in size.

For the next month, Mark checked the nest. The father bird continued his assigned task. Except for his nightly sojourn for food, he remained on the nest. Constant communication among Mark, Gail Barnes of the wildlife center in Lubbock, and us was vital to the outcome. When Mark reported, "Two hatched," then later, "Two more," we worried if the male could feed all six if the remaining eggs were successful.

When we accepted an invitation to come and see the foursome, Mark introduced us to Gary Austin, chief mechanic for the B-29 "Fifi." Both men were excited about the CAF "family," and recalled that they had first noticed the parent owls weeks earlier. Provided with a portable steel ladder, we climbed about twenty feet, then stepped carefully onto the door assemblage and approached the nest.

Only the curved edge of the horizontal steel beam kept eggs or nestlings from plummeting to the floor below. Unbelievable was the lack of a nest. Mostly debris from pulverized pellets, rabbit hair, and the remains of mice and rats littered the beam. Essentially, the eggs had been laid on cold steel, and the youngsters had nothing to push against in their efforts to stand. Their legs would be splayed and underdeveloped if this continued.

Not long after our visit, Mark reported, "We have six!" With the age of the nestlings ranging from two and a half weeks to a few days old, the decision to intervene was made. A single parent would eventually be unable to obtain enough food for an increasingly hungry family.

Arriving at the hangar, we saw Mark and Gary with a cardboard box. Earlier, they had climbed to the nest and gathered the nestlings. When we opened the box, the familiar whimpering sound of baby owls greeted us. The four oldest had graduated from their fuzzy, white down to a woolly, buff-colored down. The remaining two were rather bedraggled and hardly larger than baby chicks.

Once the nestlings were placed in our incubator, we headed to Lubbock. Stopping in Lamesa, I checked on the babies. The four oldest were enjoying their soft, warm environment. Startled at the appearance of the youngest, I knew their fate even before handling them. Cold, with distended abdomens, their lives had been too brief.

As we continued the drive, I tried to figure out what had gone wrong, what should I have done. With no answers, we arrived at the center. From the look on my face, Gail knew something had happened. Handling each of the newly born, she reassured me that there was nothing anyone could have done to save them. Infection in the umbilical cords and malnutrition had claimed the tiny lives.

After returning home, I called Mark to relate the outcome of our efforts. He was not surprised by the news of the two youngest owls. As he and Gary had carefully gathered the nestlings, they had wondered if those babies could make it. They were so different from the older ones at that same age. Both men were relieved to learn that the surviving four could be raised by surrogate parent owls. To know they would eventually "earn their wings" made Mark feel that he had done something good. Soon the owls were just memories, until August.

As he walked toward the 40-gallon trash barrels near the north doors of the hangar, Mark jumped when he first heard a high-pitched scream. Daring to look in each container for this eerie sound, he was greeted by a heart-shaped head and small black eyes. Hissing harshly and swaying from side to side, the young barn owl lowered its head and extended its wings.

At this moment, Mark realized that the father owl must have been successful in attracting another mate and having a second family. When this youngster had attempted to leave the area above, it had only enough strength to break its fall. Instead of gliding to the floor below, it had muddled its solo flight into a trash bin. Unable to fly out of this narrow, round prison, the feathered but not flight-worthy creature had to wait for someone to find it. Thinking he could reach in and grab the bird, Mark learned in a hurry that the fledgling would throw itself on its back and strike at him with both feet.

We were happy to help a second time. After pulling the screaming owl from the barrel, I noticed its feathers were coated with a gritty, oily substance. At the wildlife center, they christened the newest CAFer, "Pigpen." Since he ate like a pig and was as dirty as the cartoon character, he was aptly named. Put with surrogate parents named "Mean" and "Nasty," the youngster would have nothing to do with them. When five more youngsters were placed in the mew to be nurtured, Pigpen positioned himself between the new arrivals and the surrogates. Once Nasty pummeled him with her one good wing, he decided to help the adult feed the younger ones, but intentionally kept Mean away. How anything so vulnerable could become so formidable was nature's secret.

33. Black-crowned Night Heron

Nycticorax nycticorax

"You'd better let me take you out there, 'cause you'll never find it by yourself," was the game warden's advice. An hour later, we headed north into the countryside. Leaving Highway 87 behind, we traveled at least two more miles before coming to a caliche road. As we headed east, the barren acres of cotton fields had no sign of wildlife until we spotted a badger. When the varmint noticed our slowing truck, it slunk until its belly dragged the bottom of a furrow. It kept going.

Turning into the driveway, we stopped at a warm and inviting farmhouse. Greeted by a chorus of dogs and the owner, we felt welcome. "It was sittin' up there in the peach tree," said the farmer. "After it sailed to the ground, it couldn't take off again. It just can't fly," he continued. "C'mon, I'll show you where it is."

On the north side of the house was a long, narrow cage. To get to the short-necked, stocky bird at the opposite end meant crawling on my knees, hunched over, with little room to spare. "Good thing it's you and not me," chuckled the game warden. It was obvious to all of us that he would never have been able to get in the cage. "When I tried to get that bird out of that thing, it just held on with its feet. 'Fraid it'd hurt itself if I kep' at it," offered the farmer. When I had first seen the bird, I knew I'd have to be very careful. Aggressive toward members of its own family of birds, it would be dangerous to approach.

Eighteen inches wide, twenty-four inches tall, the six-foot-long cage made me wonder about its use. As I squeezed into the entrance, the wire mesh on the bottom bit into my knees. It was going to be a long crawl.

Carrying my burnt-orange beach towel, I hoped to present a curtain between the bird and me. About two feet from it, I felt the first of many strikes by its sharp-pointed bill. To lower the towel slightly in order to see the position of the bird would make my eyes an easy target. Since the bird's only choice was to confront me, it did.

The first blow glanced off the right side of my forehead. As I tried to parry each forward thrust, the bird had the advantage. Ducking down to look around the edge of the towel resulted in the tip of the beak hitting the right lens of my glasses. With plastic lenses becoming the vogue, I had held on to my old, heavy safety-glass pair, which now bore the scratch intended for me. The lunge that hit my knee was my opportunity to grab the bird's bill. As it struggled against my grasp, I wrapped the towel securely around the bird, and started backing out of the cage.

Nearly out of breath from the one-sided fencing match, I slowly removed the towel. The striking black cap, red eyes, lush white underparts, yellow legs, and soft gray wings and tail, were the prominent colors of a black-crowned night heron. Extending from the back of its head were three long, narrow, white nuptial plumes that graced this handsome water bird.

"What's it doin' here?" asked the farmer. While most herons at sunset would be flying toward a nightly roost, the black-crowned had left its daytime perch to feed. From dusk until sunrise, the bird could avoid competition from other herons. While heading north, the heron, whose natural habitat would include wetlands, rivers, and marshes, had sought any bodies of water for its food. Over land devoted to agriculture, the bird had foraged for mice, insects, and earthworms. The farmer's peach tree had

offered the migrating heron a safe roost for the day. Unfortunately, it must have bruised or fractured a wing as it landed.

Once at our home, the night heron continued his surly behavior. His nearly four-foot wingspan, chunky body, and thick black-pointed bill demanded respect. Since we did not have any frogs, fish, bird eggs, or snakes on hand, we offered mice. Because he refused to eat, we had to force-feed him for a few days. The serrated beak was nature's excellent way for the bird to capture and hold its prey while shaking it into submission or death. For us, it was a challenge to nourish the heron without having our hands cut to shreds.

Having made arrangements with the wildlife center, I took the heron to work with me the next day, so that I could leave as soon as possible. During the morning, my employer arrived and was interested in the bird. "What does it eat?" he asked. Hearing of the diet prompted another comment. "How does it eat?" When I told him the bird would swallow its food whole, he gasped. "You mean it doesn't have any teeth?" Resisting the urge to laugh, I showed him the bird's large gaping mouth, and the razor-sharp edges of its mandibles. Ashen, my boss slowly backed away from the now-wiggling bird.

The good news from the wildlife center was no fractures of any bones. With time, the bird would fully recover. Once again, with strong, swift wing beats, head sunken in line with its back, legs trailing behind, the black-crowned night heron would be silhouetted against a darkening sky.

34. AMERICAN KESTRELS

Falco sparverius

ANTICIPATING A LONG DAY, he left the city at 5:00 a.m. An hour and a half later, as he crossed the cattle guard, the first hint of morning arrived. From quite a distance he could see the lights were on in the barn. "Cook" would have the coffee made.

After he had gathered his tools and apron from the truck, the farrier made his way past the horse stalls and equipment. Reaching his designated area, he noticed someone had piled hay nearby. Soon, other men who would be helping with the day's chores joined him and the cook.

HANDING HER REINS TO A WORKER WHO HAD COME TO HELP, HE WALKED TOWARD THE NEST THAT HAD BEEN WRENCHED FROM THE RAFTERS. INSIDE WERE FIVE NESTLINGS.

Having set up, the craftsman was ready for his first customer. As the quarter horse was led toward him, both man and horse recognized each other. Whether the farrier had fit a polo pony or shod a Shetland, he established a lasting rapport with the animal. Over the years, owners had commented on how their horses seemed to know he was coming.

Some time during the morning, as he cleaned another foot, he noticed a shadow moving swiftly across the barn floor. By the time he could look up, there was nothing to see. "Probably a pigeon," he thought.

By early afternoon, he decided to take a break. His arms and back were beginning to complain. Stretching and getting the kinks out, he noticed nearby some welding equipment that had been stored in the barn. He did not recognize the burly ranch hand standing next to it.

Once more, he bent beside another horse. His gentle touch allowed him to lift the horse's lower leg. As he began to work, a loud voice behind him complained, "Messin' all over the place." Before he could turn to see what was happening, he heard scuffling and smelled dust being kicked up from the barn floor. "Umph!" cried the voice behind him as a high-pitched sound of alarm echoed, "Klee, klee, klee."

As he started to rise, he heard a pole hit the ground and saw what might be a bird's nest land in the pile of hay. Turning to look at whoever was causing such a ruckus, he noticed he was not alone in staring at the stranger, who yelled, "What'd you expect me to do?" No one answered.

With every face turned in his direction and making a silent judgment, the stranger stomped out of the barn. His profane analysis of the barn, everyone in it, and the birds was heard until he slammed his truck door and created his own dust storm in leaving.

When the nest had landed in the hay, the horse moved backward, then forward repeatedly in terror at the stranger's shouting curses. Talking to the horse, the farrier finally managed to calm the frightened mare. Handing her reins to a worker who had come to help, he walked toward the nest that had been wrenched from the rafters. Inside were five nestlings.

Showing the downy, partially feathered youngsters to the men, the farrier recognized the birds as American kestrels. "All that guy had to do was move," said Cook. "Why'd he go and do somethin' like that!"

Two of the ranch hands had witnessed the courtship of the parents. "You should'a seen it. The daddy brought her some food while she was in that mesquite tree. She wouldn't take it. He offered it again. She ignored him. Even dropped it on the ground. He picked it up, brought it back a third time, and she took it. From then on, they've been together."

After the eggs hatched, the men had seen the daily trips made by the parents. Hunting in the morning and late afternoon, the birds had shrunk the thriving mice colony at the barn. The countryside provided an endless supply of grasshoppers. Accustomed to their goings and comings, the ranch hands had forgotten about the birds, until now. Asking the farrier what he planned to do with the kestrels, they were told he was going to call a "bird lady" and see if she could help. To know that something could be done for the now-homeless beings was gratifying.

On his way back to the city, the farrier delivered the kestrels to us. Apparently healthy, hungry, and safe after their unexpected relocation, the nestlings would soon be taken to a wildlife center. Placed with adult kestrels, they would learn to catch and kill their prey. Release to the wild would follow when they were flight-worthy.

Kestrels had often reminded us of a child holding an ice cream cone. Given a natural dexterity with their talons, they would always first position food so as to eat the most delicious part. Bites would be taken off the head, then the rest of their prey, whether they were insects, mice, lizards, or small birds. Any food remaining on their talons would gingerly be picked off. Finally, just as a kid would wipe his mouth on his sleeve, they would clean their beaks by rapidly brushing them back and forth across their perch.

The kestrels' first flight had occurred as a downward spiral. When mature, their wingspread of nearly twenty-four inches would enable them to hover and glide on narrow pointed wings. Someday, they might also choose a more natural setting, such as a tree cavity or hillside outcropping, when starting their own families.

KESTRELS HAD OFTEN REMINDED US OF A CHILD HOLDING AN ICE CREAM CONE.

35. Great Horned Owls – "Virginia"

Bubo virginianus

BEGINNING WITH SMALL STICKS AND twigs, she carefully placed them in the crotch of a large elm. After pulling buff-colored down from her breast, she placed the feathery cushion among and on top of the crisscrossed wood. This would be the scant lining for her nest.

Chosen for its natural hollow, the elm near the cistern had served for over ten years as a nest site by the great horned owl family.

As the tree began to bud and leaf out, she was constantly brooding, during cold and stormy weather, the three eggs she had laid. Instinctively,

she knew to keep the center of the nest dry and warm.

Nestled and almost hidden from a distance by numerous stately elms, the ranch home attracted wildlife because of water. Spending the weekend in the solitude offered by the vast sections of open land, the owner noticed the nest as she walked outside to sit on the porch. "Looks like we're going to have another family," she mused.

The human family had enjoyed watching this yearly event, and had even photographed the nest and its young from a second-story window. One year, after a cold, wet spell, nestlings had died because water had been trapped in the crook of the tree. A drainage pipe was installed to insure that, in the future, the nest would remain dry during adverse weather conditions. Weeks passed. A phone call from the ranch confirmed there were three young in the nest.

With the morning sun warming the nestlings, the mother owl could finally rest after a night of hunting. Keeping her ravenous babies supplied with food was a constant challenge. Fortunately, mice, rats, and cottontail rabbits were plentiful. As the avian family settled for a long day's sleep, the mother, partially hiding her young, seemed to blend into the bark. Nature had given her the necessary camouflage to protect both herself and her family.

The more the owl hunted mice near the ranch house, the more she brought attention to herself. Leaving the nest and flapping her great wings, she would sail low over the lawn and close to the hedge just outside the porch. Mice would scurry to avoid her sharp talons, but her reflexes and keen vision were not to be denied.

One evening her silent, swift flight was interrupted by the ranch dog coming from the east side of the yard. Barking, the blond canine, that greeted everyone to the ranch, charged at the owl as she grabbed an errant rat and flew back up to the tree. As it stood on its hind legs in an effort to reach the nest and the trespassing creature, the dog continued to bark. The man and his wife, who live behind the ranch house, decided to check on the dog. After seeing it at the base of the tree, they realized it was barking because the owl was hunting in its territory. With the bird unreachable, they thought the dog would settle down and that would be the end of it.

During several more nights, the performance was repeated. Each time the man or woman checked on the front yard, the dog was yelping at the mother owl. On several occasions, they had seen the great horned owl swoop down and grab a chunk of hair from the dog's back. Soon, he'd find a rabbit to chase and forget about the bird. One night, however, the barking continued longer than normal. Fearing that a different creature might be outside, the man knew he'd better see what was there.

Entering the front yard, he noticed that the great horned owl was on the grass. As she popped her bill, the dog would bark, start forward, then back up as loud, numerous hoots came from her throat. The owl's large head and glaring yellow eyes made the dog tremble. With her prominent ear tufts straight up, her white throat patch swelling with each "Hoo, hoo," and her legs extended with open feet warning of sharp talons, she reminded the dog that it had better keep its distance. As he grabbed the dog's collar to pull it back from the owl, the man noticed the bird's injured wing. He figured the dog had turned abruptly when attacked by the owl, and had succeeded in disabling his tormentor.

After he locked the dog in his back yard, the man returned. To look again at the twisted extremity made his stomach churn. Knowing he could not leave the owl on the ground, he went to the barn for a large animal trap. His gloved hands picked up the protesting owl and placed it inside. In the morning, he'd call the owner to get help for the mother and the three nestlings left in the tree.

"The mother owl is injured. She can't hunt, and the babies need to be fed," came the desperate plea from the owner. After being advised by the director at South Plains Wildlife Center in Lubbock to bring the three chicks and the mother as soon as possible, we headed to the ranch.

A look at the owl's injured wing told us that it could not be repaired. Once I was able to get the bird out of the trap, we placed her in a large dog carrier with the nestlings that I had taken from the tree.

Grateful to the owner and her husband for taking the owl family to the wildlife center, we learned that a decision had been made regarding the owl's wing. If the mother were to remain with her young during the important months of their development, the wing would require amputation. After that time, the center would allow her to become a surrogate parent to orphaned great horned owls. Finding a name for this addition to the center, volunteers decided to use a portion of the Latin name for the great horned owl: bubo virginianus. While bubo depicts the genus of owls, virginianus designates the locale from which the first member of the species was scientifically collected. They would call this new mother, "Virginia."

Placed in a mew after her surgery, Virginia and her offspring adopted their new home. Allowed the privilege of raising her young, the owl fed them mice and rats provided daily by the volunteer staff. She taught them some of the skills needed for existing in the wild. When the young were flying, the time came for them to be placed in the large flight cage in order to develop muscle tone and strength.

With her maternal work at an end, Virginia suddenly went into a decline and started to peck and tear the area where her wing had been removed. Having seen this behavior before in amputees, the director and manager decided that the continued damage to tissue and nerves, and the ensuing infections, meant the owl would have to be euthanized.

"She knew her job was done. That's nature," commented the ranch owner upon hearing the reasons why the mother owl's life was terminated. Although Virginia would not return to the ranch, her offspring were brought back for release. For four to five days, they were housed in a stable retrofitted as a release site. When they were deemed ready, the doors were blocked open in the evening, and the threesome left to start new homes on the ranch.

36. Chihuahuan Ravens

Corvus cryptoleucus

To the lineman, it seemed the restless flocks were arriving earlier each spring. As he drove countless miles inspecting the system, he noticed numerous nests in mesquite and hackberry. Where there were no trees, windmill towers and the cross-arms of utility poles sufficed. Year after year, the birds used the same nest. By early June there would be young.

Stopping to watch the annual courtship, he loved to see his favorite duo standing side by side atop their pole. As they rubbed their bills together, they would bow, and then raise their wings. Ruffled and exposed by a gust of wind, the feathers of their throats and upper necks would suddenly appear as white boas against the glossy purplish-black feathers that normally hid them.

Built by the female, the nest was a bulky, round mass of thorny twigs. He guessed it must be at least twenty inches across. More than once after nesting season ended, he had removed a Chihuahuan raven's nest because of problems on the line. Inside the nests were remnants of cattle hair, grass, rabbit fur, rags, bits of rope, and newspaper. He marveled at the female's ability to interlace twigs, sticks, and rusty, cast-off wire into a safe, deep haven for her young.

Sometime after midnight, the constant ringing of the phone awakened him. In a way, he had anticipated being called. The unexpected front, with its lightning and thunder, had brought high winds and a cold, steady rain. By dawn he would be back in the same sector he had checked more than a month ago.

As he approached the pole, he noticed the raven's wing extending beyond the edge. Having seen the parents and their broods for years, he felt uneasy. The noise of his truck and his shutting the door caused no movement by the large black bird. When the bucket had carried him slightly above the cross-arm, he looked down and was startled. Sprawled atop her nest, the lifeless female raven completely covered any young or eggs from his sight. Lowering the bucket enough to examine the lower part of the nest, he noticed a piece of barbed wire extending from the structure. During the turbulent storm, an integral part of the nest that had held it together had somehow worked loose and made contact with the line. Her movements to shield her family had resulted not only in causing a short circuit, but her electrocution.

Lifting the valiant mother, the lineman found wiggling nestlings huddled together. The youngest appeared to be a few days old. Much larger was the oldest. All had gaping mouths waiting to be fed. Since the remaining parent could not keep them warm and secure food at the same time, the man decided to take the youngsters.

When he called his wife, she was not too surprised. His travels through open country often resulted in his bringing home a critter for her to raise. This time was different. She didn't have a clue as to what to feed five baby ravens.

Although storms can be an indication of incoming birds, we never expected this challenge. After asking the lady to keep the babies warm, we started the 25-mile trip to her home. Gray skies still threatened to rain, and northeasterly winds buffeted our vehicle. We hoped the nestlings had not been exposed to the elements for too long a time. Inviting us inside, the lady mentioned she was in the process of trying to feed the infants. Anticipating a messy ordeal, she had placed the five babies on a tile floor. With nothing to push against, the ravens had wallowed in the food that had missed their mouths.

As I picked up the smallest, I realized how chilled it was. Since nestlings are naked at first, two of the young had nothing to retain body warmth. Only the older three had started developing a brownish-gray down. Asking the lady to thank her husband and telling her how much we appreciated her calling us, we started home. When we were far enough away, we stopped to rearrange our passengers. Placing the five inside my shirt, I knew body heat was the quickest way to warm young life. Quickly, the quintet grew comfortable and slept the rest of the way.

Knowing that Chihuahuan ravens have both animal and vegetable diets, we researched long enough to discover that the nestlings are nearly entirely carnivorous. Thus, minced mice from sunup to sundown were provided for the protein and calcium they needed. Naturally, the largest nestling ate the most. We carefully monitored the intake of the smallest ones to make sure all of the birds were well-fed. Warmth and diet soon made a difference. The ravens seemed to grow as we fed them, and being satisfied, they slept soundly until the next feeding. Increasingly vocal with guttural sounds, one would awaken and sound the hunger alarm for the others. When we took the nestlings to the wildlife center, volun-

teers were eager to supply the demands of these deep-voiced creatures.

Feeding the nestlings and knowing what they could become, we were transported back in time to a fall migration. On the winding mountain roads of Colorado and New Mexico, we had accompanied flocks cavorting as they traveled. Sideways somersaults resulted in some of the ravens flat on their backs in the air. Quickly, they recovered themselves with another turn. These aerial antics by nature's clowns endeared us to the specie. We never dreamed that some day we would be responsible for five emerging lives.

37. Red-tailed Hawks

Buteo jamaicensis

Circling high above the red and white microwave tower, the large bird of prey had a commanding view of its nest and the surrounding countryside. With our vehicle slowly coming to a stop, we lowered the windows and watched it soar on that hot summer afternoon. We could easily spot a large nest located on the top of the mount for one of three communication dishes.

Called to identify the family of birds that had claimed the tower as a nest site, we knew by the raptor's size and the chestnut red on the upper side of its tail that red-tailed hawks were the occupants.

The guy wires that had insured the tower would remain erect had lost much of their tension. High winds or thunderstorms could cause the tower to fall. Wanting to replace the wires and service the tower, the pipeline company was aware of the federal laws regarding nesting birds. U. S. Fish & Wildlife required that, in addition to identification, a designated wildlife rehabilitator be contacted. When we met with a representative that afternoon, we discussed the options.

With our binoculars, we confirmed that there were two nestlings in the makeshift aerie. To allow them to remain in their nest until feathered enough to fly would be the ideal solution. Planned studies of the guy wires, however, might change this scenario. Everyone agreed to await the results.

As we watched the twosome anticipate their parent and feeding, we marveled at how they instinctively stayed within the boundaries of the nest's edge. Only woven sticks indicated a limit to their activities.

Three weeks later, the call came. Instead of having 1,600 pounds of tension on the wires, a little over a fourth of that was evident. If the tower and lines were not serviced immediately, a potential failure could be catastrophic for both the tower and the nestlings.

Weather and wind would be factors in our accessing the tower. While the pipeline company made arrangements for a crane, we contacted federal and state authorities. With a calm morning forecast the next day, we realized we were about to experience one of our highest rescues.

When we arrived at the tower, the crane was in place. Positioning of the huge equipment was critical, since the cage attached to the cables was between the various guy wires. To keep it from striking the tower would take constant communication between the crane operator and an employee inside the cage.

"One of 'em didn't make it," said a man who took us to the fence surrounding the base of the tower. Lying on the ground were the remains of one of the nestlings. We had watched the birds the previous day. Sometime during the night, the bird had either been knocked or taken from the nest. Downy, with emerging feathers, the young hawk could have plummeted to its death, or been an owl's evening meal. We'd never know.

As I started to turn away, a man moved the carcass with the toe of his boot. Then he stooped to pick it up and toss it away from the site. Thoughts of that first day when we saw the energetic twosome made me regret waiting to give nature and the birds their chance. Yet I knew deep inside it was the right decision. The most important thing to accomplish now was to save its sibling. Concentrate on that, I told myself repeatedly.

Due to concern that the operator and I might be attacked by the mother hawk, our hosts required us to wear hard hats, jackets, and a harness. Realizing how large the cage was and asking about its capacity, I requested that

Art come along. "He can read my mind before I say it. I'll need him up there," was my plea. Coming aboard, Art was to be invaluable.

As the cage started upward, the female red-tail circled the tower. With no wind, I could hear her raspy scream, Kree-e-e-e. From below, she appeared white, with brown streaks on her lower neck and dark streaking across her belly. As she turned, her wingspread of nearly five feet was awesome.

Slowly, carefully, the cage continued to rise. Art was ready at any moment to keep it from touching the tower. Any additional noise or commotion could cause the nestling to jump. To get my thoughts together for what we had to do, I looked out at the countryside. The remains of foundations from an oil camp many years ago became more evident as we climbed. Looking toward the horizon, I could see a ranch home, windmills, and sections of mesquite, juniper, cactus, and native grasses. It was a restful respite after such a harsh discovery.

Inch by inch, or so it seemed, the cage arrived at the bracket supporting the nest. Uncertain of what it was seeing, the nestling appeared skittish. Having brought some beef heart, I thought of offering it to the hawk. "Get the net over it now. You don't have that much time. It could jump," whispered Art. "You may only have one chance." Leaning over the edge of the cage while he held it a few inches from the tower, I moved the net slowly into position.

With one hand on the tower and the other grabbing my belt from behind, Art allowed me to stretch another few inches. Down went the net over the young hawk. It jumped violently upward. Having the bird pinned to the nest by the force of the netting and its rim, I called, "It's in the net! Hold me right where we are." Wiggling a few inches further outside the cage, I was able to get my free hand under the net. Grabbing one leg, then the other, I sighed, "Pull me and the net back in the cage. We have a hawk."

Once inside with my feet on the floor, I could let Art help remove the net from the nestling. Placed inside a pillowcase and pressed against my side, the hawk calmed as we started down. After showing the young red-tail to the supportive pipeline and crane workers, we took our young charge to the wildlife center in Lubbock. There it became fully feathered, capable of strong flight, and developed the ability to find and kill its food.

Seven weeks later, with the pipeline representatives present, the juvenile hawk was released a few hundred yards from the tower. Pointing the release box toward an ancient mesquite, we opened the door and the red-tail left like a bullet. After landing high in the tree, the raptor took its time in examining its new terrain. With strong flaps of its wings, the hawk headed north. Rising to greet it from a distant clump of trees was an adult red-tail. Together they discovered each other, and last seen were still flying north.

38. HARRIS'S HAWK

Parabuteo unicinctus

Having found the bird of prey as she walked her dog, the woman had thrown her blouse around it and headed for her house. As she related later, "Fortunately, no one saw me in my bra." Once home, she decided to keep the young hawk in the bathroom. It could at least go from the floor, to the commode, to the rod once she removed the shower curtain. The mess the bird would make could easily be cleaned, although it would occasionally have to share the accommodation with her.

A cheerful greeting, "Hi, this is Kathy," had been my introduction to Mrs. Semeniuk. After asking for her address and phone number, I mentioned the spelling of her name. "Don't worry about that. It's just as hard to spell it as to say it. Just call me Kathy."

When she found the hawk about a half-block from her home, she sensed something might be wrong with the bird, since it did not take flight as she approached. Aware of the large flock of hawks that had nested in the clump of trees at the end of the street, Kathy realized that the bird could have hatched during late April. Although seemingly on its own, the juvenile

may not have been successful in its attempt to become an active hunter of small birds and mammals. It might still be dependent upon its parents for food. After numerous inquiries, Kathy contacted us. Since she did not own a car, we agreed to come to Monahans in Ward County to get the hawk.

As we walked through Kathy's home, her various pets were evident. Each had its own place. Whether exotic birds or newborn puppies, cleanliness mattered. To have a raptor in the restroom was new for her.

When we slightly opened the bathroom door and squeezed inside, a first-year-young Harris's hawk was perched on the rod above the tub. Only a few months had passed since it had occupied a nest in the very trees under which it was found. In addition to sticks, twigs, and weeds, its parents had lined its first home with leaves, grass, and the fresh new growth from neighboring mesquites. From soft down to its juvenile plumage, it had the conspicuous markings of its species. Even at this early age, the hawk had emerging coloration on its shoulders, mottled chest, white rump, and long, white-tipped tail. As it matured, its body and head would be covered by dark brown feathers, along with prominent, rufous wing coverts and thighs. Someday, the bird could easily be described as a "red hawk."

Unaccustomed to our presence, the hawk jumped from the rod to the top of the commode. From there it quickly darted behind "the convenience" like a dog before a storm. Although the room was small, it proved a challenge in trying to grab a hawk that easily evaded us by going from one side to the other. Finally, with my hands on either side of the commode, I had the bird contained. With Art blocking one side, I shifted to the other and managed to grab the wayward youth.

Bringing the hawk from his narrow hiding place, I held him over the tub until Art could open the carrier. Once the bird was inside, I had a chance to look around the room. The bottom of the tub looked like the worst of modern art. The patience and willingness of Kathy to house and feed the hawk until we could arrive deserved many kind words.

Four days later, the hawk was delivered to the wildlife center. About a month and a half passed. When it was finding and killing its food, and had become quite adept at flying, the Harris's was given back to us for release. For this bird of southwestern border regions and arid plains to be successful, it needed an area for open hunting and few people.

After giving the Harris's hawk a send-off breakfast of mice and beef heart, we took it fifteen miles south of Monahans to an area of greasewood, wild flowers, spindly grasses, and cactus. Cottontail rabbits, lizards, mice, and small birds were abundant. Flying about a hundred yards after gaining its freedom, the bird settled on the ground near a thick clump of desert scrub. As it surveyed its surroundings, a mockingbird discovered the uninvited visitor to its territory. With welcoming pecks on the raptor's head, the feisty songbird flew away quickly after letting the bird of prey know alertness is the key to survival.

39. Barn Swallows

Hirundo rustica

As they winged their way northward, the couple left behind a South American winter. As others joined them, their flock crossed the Rio Grande. When they finally arrived at the two-storied motel, last year's home was awaiting them.

Inspecting what the cleaning lady had often called a "cup of mud," the twosome was relieved at not having to build another nest. Two years prior to this spring morning, they had labored tirelessly in gathering the building materials from nearby mud puddles and open fields. While some birds would carry each small pellet of mud pressed against their forehead on top of their bills, these parents had preferred to carry the wet earth in their mouth and throat. Mixing pieces of dry grass with the mud, the birds looked as if they were squeezing cookie dough from an applicator. The mud would ooze into place on one of the many rows it took to erect the high wall that would protect their eggs and young. It had taken nearly two weeks to finish tapping each glob of mud into place with their bills.

Since no repairs were needed for their summer home, the pair began to fly swiftly, as if in a hurry. Constant twittering could be heard throughout the day. Landing on the upstairs railing that covered the length of the motel in front of each room, the female began to twitch her wings and tail. After the male landed close beside her, they rubbed their heads and necks together. After interlocking their bills, they preened each other's plumage.

After the courtship, the couple searched for feathers to line the nest. Soon, it was obvious that incubation had begun. Each shared this duty as well. In a little over two weeks, the parents were seen rushing in and out of the nest. A family had begun.

Asking for the key to a familiar room on the motel's second floor, we were grateful for a brief vacation in the rugged mountains of southwest Texas. Since we were able to access and hike remote ranches, we anticipated the beautiful sunsets and wildlife we would encounter. As we approached our unit, we noticed ahead a pile of debris on the concrete porch.

Suddenly, whizzing past our heads in frenzied flight were two barn swallows. As they landed on the side of what had been their earthen home, we briefly saw the tiny heads of their offspring peering over the edge. When they weren't diving at us, the parents would return to check on their young. Somehow, their mud nest had come apart from atop the door frame to our room.

Sensing the urgency of their plight, we put our gear in the room and tried to decide how to help. The best solution would be to reattach the nest to the building and let the parents raise the nestlings. Since it was early afternoon, few people had checked in for their stay. We felt the nest would be safe for a brief time.

After talking with the manager/owner of the motel, we learned how treasured these swallows were. Guests for many years had enjoyed their company and antics. Only when the birds had migrated would any deteriorating structures be removed. "Our swallows are part of our attraction. They're good for business," shared the lady who had given us our key. When we told her that we would secure the nest in its same location, she seemed relieved.

A visit to the hardware store supplied our needs. Back at the motel, we worked quickly. Taking the babies out of the nest, we first used an epoxy to cement one part back to the main body of the mud cup. Following that

Placing the nestlings back in their home, we went downstairs and into the parking lot. We did not have long to wait. Since the parents had stayed close to the motel, they immediately flew to their young once we were away. Soon the adults were scurrying in and out with fresh, small insects. This activity would continue until dusk.

Each morning as we started our walk to breakfast, we were greeted by the twittering chatter of the parents. The nestlings hung their heads out over the edge of the nest as if nothing had happened. When we returned after a day's outing, the adults would be perched on the nest as if they were the proudest of parents. Although the mud cup had been slightly altered, they accepted our effort.

Over the days we were there, we were able to closely view the colorful parents. A metallic bluish-black above, with reddish-brown forehead and breast, the male beneath was a faint cinnamon-cream. His mate was slightly duller in color. Both had deeply forked tails. As they caught food in flight for their babies, they truly exhibited the joy of flying.

was a coarse twine that we wove into a mesh to surround the exterior of the cup. By standing on chairs, we could reach the top of the door frame. Our support structure was long enough that we were able to nail its overlapping length to the wall. This would have to compensate for the jarring of the wall every time the door opened and closed. It was no wonder the nest had collapsed. The swallows' natural plaster could last only so long.

To the parents, the nest would appear to be in the same place. Since birds do not have a developed sense of smell, they would never know their young had been anywhere but in the nest. It was time to test our theory.

40. Northern Mockingbird vs. Western Kingbird

Mimus polyglottos & Tyrannus verticalis

YEAR ROUND, HER DOMAIN WAS NOT only the live oak in the front yard, but the entire side and back of our property. Squirrels, migratory intruders, and cats were never spared from the songbird's diving attacks. With her nestlings demanding an abundance of insects, the mockingbird would constantly be seen swooping from the nest, crossing in front of the garage, and heading toward her mainstay, our natural side yard and the honeysuckle on an intermediate fence.

Unknown to our permanent resident, a western kingbird had constructed her nest atop the transformer that was mounted on a utility pole behind our back fence. To the untrained eye, both nests were quite similar. Using twigs, grasses, and stems of castaway weeds, the two females had created safe family homes in which to raise their young. While the nest in the oak tree was hidden in dense foliage to protect the eggs and nestlings, the other abode offered the pole's shade from the hot, afternoon sun. A good view of easement, back and side yards, and the undeveloped lots to the east was required for this member of the flycatcher family.

When the season for courtship had begun, the differences in the species were evident. Running across our front lawn, the male mockingbird would flit his tail up and down. While making a cooing sound, he would lift and spread his wings high above his back, then outward to display his large white wing patches. With the female crouching and quivering her wings, we knew the season would be entertaining.

Flying upwards, then suddenly tumbling in the air, the male kingbird had repeated his aerial display again and again. Enhancing his show with a shrill cry, he even somersaulted backwards. As he made his presence and intentions known, the adept insect eater flashed the red crown patch normally hidden by the gray feathers on top of his head. With his chosen agreeable, the courtship had been successful.

Since both species were dependent upon insects for themselves and their young, the parents were diligent in their pursuit of food. While the mockingbirds hunted for bugs under leaves, and pecked worms, moths, grasshoppers, and butterflies from shrubbery, the kingbirds captured insects, including dragonflies, in flight. When desperate, both species would consider wild fruit.

As the young grew and feathered, the search for food intensified. Inevitable was the meeting of one specie in the other's territory. Sailing out into the air from either the oak tree or the power line, a parent would dive at the offending bird. With this competition for insects, and their young out of the nest and learning to fly, we saw throughout the day streaks of gray and white chasing yellow, gray, and black, or vice versa.

Animosity grew. Having already established dominance over our home site, the mockingbird resented this migratory invasion. Bossy to extremes, the gray and white defender was furious with the kingbird. Perched on the power lines, the interloper was defiant of the mockingbird's repeated assaults.

As the fledglings learned to hunt for themselves, the adults supplemented their diet with a visit to the red berries growing wild in the side yard. Then they discovered the grape vine. To us, the fruit was too small and extremely tart. For hungry mockingbirds and kingbirds, it was a welcome change. Watching from the den windows, we saw the ultimate feud climax when the male of each specie arrived at the vine at the same time.

Assuming the offensive, the kingbird chased the mockingbird into the dense leaves. Movement of the birds could be detected by the rustling of leaves and partial sighting of thrashing colors. Soon leaves were being knocked to the ground. The mockingbird appeared, only to disappear again as it pursued its adversary. Suddenly, the leaves were still. Slowly a head poked its way clear of a cluster of grapes. Then the whole bird emerged. While it regained its bearings, we could easily enjoy the coloration of the flycatcher. Gray above and yellow-bellied below, the bird had a distinct black tail with a white feather down each side. With some feathers askew, the kingbird managed to fly back to the utility pole.

No other movement in the vine occurred. We waited. The mockingbird's head slowly appeared. Making sure that the other bird was gone, the songbird dropped to the ground. Dazed, it did not try to fly. Finally, it made an effort but could not elevate.

Hoping the warrior was only bruised and tired, we placed it in an exercise cage. After covering the disheveled bird so that it could rest, we left it for several hours. To our relief, the mockingbird was perched on the highest roost when we removed the cover. Since its family was self-reliant at this point, we kept the bird for four days on the assumption that it was sore from its experience. With each day it became more active and restless. Turning it loose in the garage, we were pleased to see it fly anywhere it wished. Recapturing it, we raised the door, walked to the oak tree, and wished it well as it hopped from limb to limb in getting away from us. Reaching the top of the tree, the guardian of our yard began its usual melodious and varied songs.

41. Northern Cardinal

Cardinalis cardinalis

Tumbling on the pavement toward the curb, he had been spared a crushing end to his life by the downdraft of the speeding truck. In the vehicle's path as he returned to his territory, the songbird never saw the approaching danger.

As she walked back to her classroom, a teacher observed the aftermath of yet another speeder in front of the school. After crossing the street, she noticed the bird was covered with sand and grit as it stood to regain its composure. When it did not fly away, she realized it was disoriented. To leave it curbside would probably result in another, more deadly, consequence.

Walking into my office, the teacher held both hands together. Even though the bird's head was covered, its long, red tail could belong only to a male cardinal. "Dazed. Absolutely out of it," were her first words. After telling of the bird's close call, she placed it in a cardboard box for such emergencies. "With time, he could recover," was my answer to her worried query about his outcome.

During the rest of the morning, no sound was heard from the box. An hour before the final bell rang that afternoon, a welcome thump, followed by footsteps, echoed from the cardinal's enclosure. His long rest had ended when he awakened to find himself in a semi-dark place. Although daylight came through the air holes, the bird did not know where he was. He proceeded to explore and escape if possible. To me, those were welcome noises and possible signs of recovery.

Before the turbulence created by the truck had flipped the cardinal to the pavement, the teacher had seen him heading toward the school. We both felt he was "ours." Every day, staff and students enjoyed the feeder outside my window. A pair of cardinals was seen frequently throughout the year.

Almost entirely red, except for the black patch of feathers surrounding the base of his large, thick bill, the male would often raise and lower his crest as if to accentuate his feelings. His mate was gray, brownish above, with reddish wings, crest, and bill. Being early to school meant one could enjoy their morning songs: whoo-ett, whoo-ett, whoo-ett; tuer, tuer, tuer. Their pret-ty, pret-ty, pret-ty aptly described their coloration and stature.

Although we never found their nest, two fledglings appeared on the ground near the feeder one summer. When the school was eerily silent because all students and teachers were in their classrooms, the male would choose one of the cars in the parking lot for his attention. Not only would he peck at his reflection in the hubcaps, but also the outside mirrors were frequently attacked.

Once home, I prepared a long cage for his journey back to nature. Sunflower seeds, cracked corn, wild bird seeds, crickets, and meal worms would be tempting morsels, along with a large bowl of water for drinking and bathing. If I were able to catch a grasshopper or cicada, perhaps the cardinal could really enjoy his captivity.

With everything ready, I reached inside the box and placed my hand around the beautiful, restless creature. As he looked around the room, I could feel a vibrant energy emitting from him that I had never felt before in other birds his size. Quick to size up the situation, he stared at me for only a second before he bit me.

Adapted to cracking seeds, the cardinal's bill was firmly pinching the thin, loose, fleshy skin that joins the base of my right thumb and the last knuckle of the index finger. Like a pair of pliers, he had suddenly grabbed a very vulnerable part of my hand. Pulling him off might cause damage. If I could stand it, I thought it better to raise my hand just enough so that his feet were barely off the floor. When he finally decided to let go because his beak was being pulled off by the weight of his body, he would not have far to fall. I waited. And waited. Nothing happened.

With no one to help, gravity and time would have to come to my rescue. As I stood there with my loose flesh holding this irate bird, I knew that no bite from a hawk or owl had ever hurt that much. Minutes passed.

Finally, he let go. Quickly grabbing him with my left hand and placing him inside the cage, I noticed he immediately flew up to a perch, turned, and glared back at me.

Having observed the cardinal for several hours, and with about an hour of daylight left, we took the bird back to the school for release. No longer confined, the cardinal easily reached the top of an Arizona cypress. Checking his territory, he then flew to other trees on the campus. With no visible injuries except to his dignity, the cardinal was more inclined to accept nature's healing rather than ours.

42. Turkey Vulture

Cathartes aura

Whether he had trouble would be up to the guy who had the birds. Having dealt with him before, the game warden was surprised at his latest adventure. In town, the rumor had circulated enough that it finally crossed his path. Having thanked the person who told him, he anticipated the confiscation of the man's latest activity.

Parking in front of the house, he couldn't imagine where the birds might be kept. A few minutes passed after he rang the doorbell. Finally, he knocked. With no response, the officer decided to leave. Having turned the corner, he parked beside a truck that was against the curb. Not having to wait very long, he noticed the front door of the residence slowly open. Through the other truck's windows, he saw the man he had come to see. Glancing from side to side, the culprit went back inside his house and closed the door.

Since he knew the man was inside the house, the warden drove to the easement. Not wanting the man to know he had returned, he left his truck and started walking down the alley. The high weeds, dilapidated outbuildings, stacks of rotting lumber, and trash hid his approach. Finally be-

hind the man's house, he saw two dark-colored birds chained in the back yard. Flies, carcasses, and waste surrounded the young juveniles.

This time he knocked on the back door. Since he thought the warden had left, the man opened the door. As he tried to shut it, the warden used his large, muscular physique to prevent its closure. "Guess you've got me this time," drawled the man. "Again," answered the warden.

"Where'd you get those vultures?" inquired the officer. If the man could be believed, the raptors had come from an abandoned barn not too far from the city. While cliffs, caves, and trees were more normal homes for the carrion eaters, the game warden had heard stories about abandoned structures being used by not only barn owls, but also turkey vultures.

Shrugging his shoulders, the man lent his expertise to the conversation by saying, "Those buzzards ain't worth nothing." With a grin on his face, the officer informed him they were probably worth a lot more than he thought.

As I drove northeast to meet the game warden, his description of the vultures had sounded as if they were about two and a half months old. When

we met, only slight evidence remained of the snowy white down on their breasts, bellies, and necks. Although their wings were developed, the naked skin of their heads and necks was a pale black. Once adult, the bare heads and necks would be a red to purple-red.

Appearing to be almost grown, the vultures were incapable of flight. After birth, it would take nearly three and a half months before their muscle tone would be adequate enough for them to become airborne. Having been chained to the ground, the birds at least had been able to sun and exercise their wings, although their legs had possible permanent markings from their confinement.

From inside the carrier came the familiar hiss of two very disgruntled vultures. Their world had changed again. Fortunately, when the man had absconded with the birds, they were ready for a solid, natural diet. If the thief had acted earlier, he would have been hard-pressed to duplicate the regurgitation of animal matter necessary for their development.

On the drive home, the two-lane road through open ranch land was the summer home to even more vultures. An occasional dead rabbit or skunk was

invitation enough for these birds to dine. With their keen eyesight and acute sense of smell, they cleared the carnage from the previous night. A song from the movie, Mackenna's Gold, came to mind: Old Turkey Buzzard… Old Turkey Buzzard…Flying, flying high…He's just awaiting…Buzzard's just awaiting…Waiting for something down below to die.

For my two passengers, a better environment meant the company of other vultures in captivity. From them, they would learn the nuances of cautiously approaching a carcass, the hesitancy of walking about the body for a while before dining to make sure it didn't move. Although awkward and downright clumsy on the ground, these scavengers-to-be could one day take flight with their long, broad wings. After learning to soar and sail for miles without a wing beat, they would truly be flying, flying high.

43. Greater Yellowlegs

Tringa melanoleuca

From the Big Spring State Park, it was visible. To try to see it from Interstate 20 was impossible. Sunken by centuries of erosion caused by the rushing runoff from seasonal thunderstorms, the salt lake offered a year-round haven. Masked by tall range grasses, acres of mesquite, and the rise and fall of the surrounding terrain, this oasis for waterfowl was, in essence, nature's secret.

Thirty-one years ago, we had approached the eastern edge of the lake to view the nightly ritual of wintering sandhill cranes. With the setting sun turning the western sky a vivid orange, the silhouettes of some 35,000 birds threatened to darken the evening sky. At that time, we had no idea that such a phenomenon would be only a memory.

When a ranch foreman called about a bird he had found, we headed to another area of Natural Dam Salt Lake. To the north, after a lengthy, slow drive on one of many dirt roads, we met the gentleman. "It's one of those birds you see along the shore," he added after thanking us for coming. "Seems kind of funny to find a live bird on Buzzard Creek!"

A major artery for incoming water from the north, the creek was a vital habitat for this migrating, shallow water bird. Often seen along coasts, small pools in salt marshes, mud flats, and along meandering creeks, the bird had found minnows, aquatic and other insects, larvae, and worms to its liking. As it had hunted the isolated edges of the creek, it had swung its long, slightly upturned bill from side to side. By this method of skimming the water, the bird had been able to pick up food during its long journey to the south. Its daily struggle for survival had been jeopardized by a broken leg.

As it lay as comfortably as possible on a pile of rags, the three of us could not help but notice its long, bright yellow legs. Although the bird was a dark grayish-brown to black above, and whitish underneath, the speckling of white on its head, long slender neck, back, wings, and breast was a predominant feature.

Carefully handing the greater yellowlegs to us, the foreman was relieved when we told him it looked like a good break. If there is one. Because of where the break had occurred, there was an opportunity to set the leg. Asking how he found it, we learned that the bird's movement on the ground had caught the man's attention. Fortunately for the yellowlegs, when it saw the foreman's vehicle approaching, its struggle to stand had led to its discovery.

From its nest site in Alaska or Canada, the greater yellowlegs had made its way to West Texas before ending its trip to Central or South America. Often mistaken for a plover or snipe, it would be spending its winter in another locale. After a veterinarian splint the leg, the shore bird was taken to a wildlife center to recover.

Months later, it was released on a conservation lake site. Protected from ground predators, the yellowlegs could walk and hunt the muddy shoreline. With its toes webbed at their base, the bird easily kept from sinking in the wettest of conditions.

When it was fully recovered and sensed the urge to migrate, the bird would be able to leave on its own. The ranchers, who had provided an environment for recovering waterfowl, no longer would hear its whistle. One morning, when the yellowlegs heard its own specie, the swift-flyer flapped its wings, extended its colorful long legs beyond its tail, and soon was lost in the clouds.

44. Great Horned Owl — "Charlie's Owl"

Bubo virginianus

Planted when the family first moved to the county the pine tree had grown into a towering giant. Anticipating the pinecones to be gathered from last week's storm, the owner looked forward to standing in its shade and listening to the wind as it hurried through the needles. When he started out the door, he paused. Under the tree on the thick mat of St. Augustine was something almost round and white.

With the movement of the fluffy ball, he realized it was a large baby bird. Having seen the parents building or repairing their nest near the top of the thirty-foot tree, he knew their spring ritual usually resulted in two offspring. Since all had previously succeeded in remaining in the nest, he wondered how this chick-like nestling had managed to arrive safely from such a height.

After glancing around and making sure he knew where the parents were, the man walked to the bundle of down. Because it couldn't be more than a month old, he knew it would be quite a while before the bird ever took its first flight. Perhaps its developing wings helped break its fall. Knowing he could not put the young-ster back in its nest and fearful of night predators, he decided the chick needed help.

When he placed the great horned owl in our care, Charlie was beaming with pride. "It doesn't seem to be hurt," he added, but still could not fathom how the baby had fallen so far without injury. "Thank the tree," I suggested. The dense needles and the closeness of the limbs had possibly allowed the chick to bounce and slide from one level to the next until plopping on the thick grass. The tree's very structure and greenery had played a part in sparing this bird.

During the time the little owl shared our home, we could feel its emerging strength as it clutched our fingers. Its white down was rapidly being replaced by a coat of buff-colored down. Its light yellow eyes readily anticipated its next feeding, and it was not bashful in grabbing minced and baby mice.

When delivering the bird to the wildlife center, we casually called it "Charlie's Owl." Soon, whenever we, or Gail Barnes, the manager, talked regarding the development of the owl, the name would be used.

Planning to use Bubo, their educational great horned owl, as the nestling's surrogate parent, Gail had us accompany her to a mew in the barn. The adult owl with her long feathery tufts (horns) glared at our intrusion. Only Gail and the youngster entered the space. After placing the nestling in a box on the floor, Gail left.

As we watched through the vertical slats, Bubo left her perch to investigate the young owl. Soon the epitome of owl parenting took place. With Bubo in the box, the nestling cuddled under her protective wing. Later that day, when we checked back with the owls, Bubo was nearly hiding the young owl. The bonding was complete. Taking over the mealtime feeding, the adult owl would raise the nestling.

Within two weeks, the youngster was twice as big. First in the wings, then on the back and tail followed by the rest of the body, the owl's plumage pushed through its downy coat. Finally, the head started to receive its share of feathers although its ear tufts the first year would be smaller.

As it started to act like an owl, the youngster often bristled its plumage, spread its wings, snapped its bill, and threatened to attack. With more time, it was flying to the lowest perches.

Soon, it mastered the highest roosts and could fly to any part of the mew. Every time we paid a visit to check on its progress, Bubo, in defense of her young, would fly at the slatted walls to try to scare us away. Her continuous deep, guttural hooting sounds were warning enough. No one but Gail, who feeds all of the owls, dared to enter.

The adult owl's acceptance of the manager seemed logical. When fresh food and water were brought, there was always a treat for Bubo. We had watched several times as Gail offered a plate of beef heart to the working parent. Then she would gather the empty dishes and leave. Bubo always received her reward.

By June, the juvenile was nearing the time when it would leave Bubo and enter the flight cage with other juveniles. Making her daily trip to replenish food and water, Gail stood beside Bubo while she ate. With her back blocking the younger owl's view of its parent, Charlie's Owl shifted its feet and crouched. Suddenly airborne, the juvenile extended its talons. In less than a second, two slashes went down the woman's cheek. As quickly as it had attacked, the juvenile was back on the roost before Gail realized the full extent of what had happened. With blood streaming down her face, she hurried out of the mew.

"It was my fault," she related to us

later. "I took my eyes off that bird, my back was turned. I know better," was the blame she placed on herself for having been lax for a moment. Fortunately, the cuts were not deep enough for stitches, but required antibiotics.

In spite of what happened, the manager continued the same routine until Charlie's Owl was moved to the flight cage with three other juveniles. Weeks later, the foursome was ready for release. East of Lubbock, where the flat acres of cotton give way to rolling ranch land and a deep canyon promises wildlife, the great horned owls gained their freedom. Noiseless in their departing flight, their ferocity would determine their very survival.

45. Black-chinned Hummingbirds

Archilochus alexandri

Before the first day of autumn, the forecast promised a change in the weather. Expecting the typical gusty winds, dust, and sweater weather, everyone looked forward to fall. With ninety-degree temperatures, the bright, sunny day gave no indication of what was to come. Toward evening, dark, threatening bluish-gray clouds stretched across the horizon. After dark, with winds punishing the trees and howling around doors, the forecast changed.

The "blue norther" was much more than the weatherman had promised. The temperature was twenty-nine degrees by midnight. At eight o'clock the next morning, the reading remained the same.

Having planted cactus and desert foliage in March and April, we grew concerned about the continued cold. Able to cover the smaller plants, we could only hope the large scrubs and trees were established enough to weather this early wintry assault.

By evening, the temperature had never risen above freezing. Another extremely cold night was due. While having breakfast the next morning, the phone rang. A janitor for an elementary school had found a hum-mingbird. Alive, but unresponsive, the bird was being kept in the office until we could arrive.

One glance inside the box made us grateful for nature's ability to save its own. Having been cold long enough, the black-chinned hummingbird had become torpid. This means of hibernation created lower respiration and circulation rates, and spared the hummer a loss of vital body fat. Once offered a constant, warmer environment, the bird would revive and be able to continue its southerly migration.

With lunch came a distraught message from the opposite part of town. Concerned about her hummingbirds, a homeowner had found a black-chinned as she refilled her feeder. Soon, it joined our first guest.

Mid-afternoon produced yet another report, and delivered was a black-chinned found inside a garage. Each of our threesome was going to be surprised when it awoke and found it had company.

By late afternoon, the temperature had finally crept toward thirty-eight degrees. We could not help but think of all the other dormant hummers that hopefully were sheltered until the Canadian front traveled further south. The warmth of a sunny day would awaken them gradually.

When the media called about this cold snap and feeders, we stressed that October 1st is an easy date to remember for bringing in the sugar water. Nature has its own encouragement to migrate for these tiny masters of the air. Plants, such as trumpet vine, honeysuckle, and red yucca, stop blooming. With their natural providers of nectar no longer available, the birds recognize that small insects are also on the decline. Even though we had experienced a straggler during the first week in November one year, we knew if it found poor accommodations, it would continue its journey.

The next morning, the blustery weather was ushered out of our area and temperatures rose rapidly. Our trio exercised and indicated they were looking forward to their freedom. With nature beckoning, the frisky hummers, without a pause, disappeared in rapid flight toward a warmer clime.

46. Red-shouldered Hawk

Buteo lineatus

The September morning had brought cooler weather. As the game warden tossed his monthly reports on the front seat of his truck, his cell phone rang. "Wink," he said dryly, as he realized his plans had to change even before he left the driveway. That town was a few miles away.

Heading northwest, he wondered about the report of a hawk standing in someone's front yard. The drive from Monahans was brief, and he easily found the residence with its unusual guest. Introducing himself to the couple waiting near the bird, he noticed that the raptor had not moved. "Been like that since we called," said the woman. "It just stands there."

Within a foot of the hawk, the warden realized how emaciated and weak it was. No resistance was given as his gloved hands pressed the bird's wings against its body. Placing it in his carrier, the officer reassured the couple that he would be taking it to a person licensed to care for migratory birds.

As he headed back to Monahans, he debated mileage and direction in seeking help for the hawk. Since he had to report to San Angelo, he could deliver the bird to Diane Tracy, who is included in both my state and federal licenses. She could evaluate and sustain the hawk until delivering it to me in Big Spring.

Part of the southeasterly drive included his assigned counties. This was an opportunity to relax. With only occasional trucks, the officer welcomed not fighting the congestion on the interstate. Once past Crane and Rankin, the familiar towns of Big Lake and Mertzon came sooner than he liked. The countryside gave way to the outskirts of San Angelo.

After calling ahead to verify that Diane would be home, the game warden delivered the red-shouldered hawk. As she examined the raptor, she immediately realized how dangerously thin it was. "How soon can we meet?" greeted me when she called.

Within an hour, she and her husband, Dale, met us in Sterling City. Our drive home was solemn. After an initial tube feeding, the hawk was more alert. Responding to minced mice, the raptor finally started eating on its own on the fourth day. Another three days assured us that it was ready for the trip to the South Plains Wildlife Rehabilitation Center in Lubbock.

The week we had shared with the red-shouldered hawk was memorable. *Buteo lineatus* accurately described this broad-winged, striped hawk. Almost two feet long, with a four-foot wingspan, the bird wore underneath, from its throat to its thighs and tail, barred colorations of brown, orange, and white. Its eyes and back were a dull brown, and it sported a reddish patch on each shoulder. With black and white barring on the wings and tail, it was a handsome, yet secretive raptor. Its overall coloration helped it blend into varied terrains.

In late spring and throughout the summer, the red-shouldered had been a bird of the woods. Wetlands, farming country, and forests had offered it nest sites and ample food. Not at all a finicky eater, the raptor availed itself of whatever the environment offered. From snakes, fish, and turtles to small birds and rodents, it was satisfied. In more open country during migration, insects, rabbits, ground squirrels, opossums, and even skunks were not ignored.

For whatever reason, the hawk, as it drifted southward, had been unable to acquire enough food to sustain it. Even a bruised wing could have caused an inability to hunt.

At the wildlife center, the bird con-

tinued to show improvement. From a mew to the flight cage was exceptionally good news. Having convinced everyone that its weight, strength, and durability had returned, the hawk was ready to catch the winds.

Between Buffalo Springs Lake and Lake Ransom Canyon, east of Lubbock, the red-shouldered hawk was released during October. From Wink to freedom, the raptor's odyssey had covered 436 miles. The bird of prey, with its wings and tail extended, would regain its graceful, soaring flight while drawing huge circles in the sky.

47. American Osprey

Pandion haliaetus

During the afternoon, the lake's surface offered a perfect reflection of clouds and shoreline. Sighted the day before, an October visitor had performed as expected. To have the opportunity to experience such an event in nature was one of the rewards of autumn.

From a distance, its long narrow wings became visible as, once again, the bird descended in a calculated glide some twenty feet above the water. Scanning the surface for its prey, it suddenly plunged downward with its wings half-closed. As it entered the water feet first with a splash, it held its wings upward. After a brief second or two, with slow heavy beats of its powerful wings, it left the surface of the lake. Clasped in its strong claws was a fish.

As the bird started to rise from the water, it carefully repositioned the wiggling catch. With the large fish pointed headfirst, the American osprey shook beads of water from its feathers before flying away to dine.

The friend, who had called about the bird of prey's fall arrival, drove from Comanche Lake to a telephone pole on the east side of town. The location had been a favorite perch for an osprey the previous year. Having spotted the bird perched on it the day before, she knew she could show us another aspect of the "fish hawk."

Soon, the osprey landed with its catch on top of the pole. With one foot holding the fish, the bird seemed to ponder whether to commence eating. Slowly, deliberately, it started to devour its dinner. Since it had flown with both feet grasping the fish, we guessed its meal to be three to four pounds. A smaller fish would have been carried by one claw. If hungry enough, the bird would eat all but the larger bones. Any indigestible parts it would eject as a pellet. The excitement of watching the fierce osprey hunt and eat was a memorable experience.

Listening to our recorded messages a few days later, we learned of a not-so-fortunate osprey from Lake Colorado City. The game warden for Mitchell County had found the raptor in shallow water. One of the bird's wings was injured.

Soon, with the officer's help, I pulled the reluctant bird from his carrier as Art carefully held the wings against the body. With its raised crest and glaring eyes, the osprey was formidable, even to us. As I held the bird, the three of us marveled at its sleek beauty. Dark brown above and clear white below, it had a distinct spotted breast. With its head mostly white, a broad black mark through its cheeks and the side of its neck gave the appearance of a mask. With black bill and claws, legs and feet a greenish-gray, the bird sported a long, barred tail. Black patches at the wrists of the wings completed its coloration.

In a family all by itself, the osprey is ranked between the Hawk Family and the Falcon Family. With curved, round claws, the bird is also equipped with rough pads on its feet to help it hold slippery fish. With keen vision and the ability to embed those claws in the back of its catch, the osprey could grab fish that swim on or near the surface.

Since we were working with the Eos Wildlife Sanctuary in Midland at that time, plans were made to deliver the osprey as soon as possible. Through experience, it had been learned that osprey, in captivity, are hesitant to eat without another osprey. Running water and fresh fish were also necessary for the bird's recovery. Without a companion, the injured bird would refuse food and decline. Knowing of a Florida rehabber who specialized in ospreys,

Eos made the arrangements with an airline that was willing to donate a free ride in hopes of saving birds of prey.

During the drive home, we discussed how privileged we had been to have handled the bird that in Latin (*Pandion haliaetus*) means sea eagle.

"At least this one had a variation in its diet," I added. Puzzled, Art didn't understand my comment until later in the evening, when he saw on my right arm a triangular-shaped cut. It was a bite I'd always treasure.

48. Mississippi Kite

Ictinia mississippiensis

STANDING ON THE CURB beside the ravine, the bird caught the attention of a passing motorist. As he turned into his driveway, the homeowner could still see the gray hawk. A car coming from the opposite direction startled the bird. As it struggled to fly out of the way, it landed on a branch of an elm tree that had grown from the floor of the gully to about five feet above street level.

Having seen this type of bird as it soared above his neighborhood during the summer, the man knew its fellow hawks had migrated near the end of August. Why it was still here

"IT'S NOT FLYING WELL," WAS HIS FIRST COMMENT REGARDING THE BIRD. "LOOKS TO ME LIKE ONE OF THOSE MISSISSIPPI KITES," HE ADDED...

in October was puzzling. He decided to call.

"It's not flying well," was his first comment regarding the bird. "Looks to me like one of those Mississippi Kites," he added. To myself, I thought "I hope not." If it were that specie, then the bird definitely had a problem.

When asked if I was familiar with the ravine, I mentioned that we had lived two houses away from it for twenty-four years. To the west of the deep drainage area lived a public school superintendent and his wife. One day, while trying to gather some trash from her side of the downward-sloping edge of the drainage easement, Mildred had lost her balance. Landing on her hip, she had slid off the abrupt vertical concrete wall to the rock-filled canyon floor. Unable to stand, she realized her leg was broken.

Having remained at the bottom for several hours before someone heard her calls for help, Mildred had cautioned the neighbors and children about the steep slopes. With her story in mind, Art and I prepared for the worst.

As we neared the ravine, we could see the kite perched on a limb in the middle of the canyon. Not only did the elm occupy this occasional source of water; every autumn we also had enjoyed the red sumac tree to the north. Mountain juniper and native scrubs created a protective cover for wildlife. For a rescue attempt, it was a tangled nightmare.

Approaching from the west, I tied a rope around my waist and a nearby tree. If I started to slide, my tether would keep me from plunging all the way to the bottom. Needing both hands to grip limbs, I proceeded to step on and over heavy foliage toward the bird. Art was to hand me the net pole once I was close enough to put it over the kite.

Another step, and the leaves and humus became slick as ice. As I started sliding downward, my hands couldn't grab limbs fast enough. A large limb loomed ahead and was my chance at stopping. When my waist slammed into the good-sized limb, I gasped for air. "Are you all right?" shouted Art. At least I was not at the end of my rope.

"Hand me the net," was my reply. For some reason, the kite had remained perched in its stoic position and watched my descent. Art and I knew this might be our only chance to net the bird. If I missed, and the kite went further into the canyon, we might never catch it.

After tightening my tether, Art then managed to thread the large net through the thick growth. Once in hand, I slowly inched toward the kite. With one foot wedged between two limbs, and leaning against my natural wooden barrier, I wasn't going any further down the slope. "Better get him," advised Art. After a forward, twisting movement, the net not only covered the hawk but ensnared its feet in the mesh. Hearing "Hurry, hurry," behind me, I pulled the wiggling hawk to my side. Even though it was tangled and struggling, the bird was ours.

To free the kite from the net required level ground. Art started pulling me and the netted bird up the slope. With only one hand free, my progress was slow. Finally out of the canyon, I was grateful to be away from nature's maze.

After freeing the kite's feet from the net, we could find no obvious fractures in its wings. Since it held them equally to the sides of its body, this beautiful summer bird might have suffered bruising or a hairline fracture. Another possibility was a toxic bug. With a diet of cicadas, grasshoppers, and crickets, the bird might have encountered a pesticide. A trip to the Lubbock wildlife center would assure that the bird would be X-rayed and examined to try to determine the cause of its late stay.

When the appropriate morning had arrived in late August or early September, this kite, for whatever reason, had been unable to depart for South America. Its light gray head with dark eye patches and red eyes turned toward us as we placed it in our carrier. The soft, darker gray of its body and the charcoal-colored wing parts gave it a striking appearance. Its gliding, soaring abilities made it an aerial champion. Because of an observant, caring person, the kite's status of being left behind, to die of starvation, changed to having another chance.

HEARING "HURRY, HURRY," BEHIND ME, I PULLED THE WIGGLING HAWK TO MY SIDE. EVEN THOUGH IT WAS TANGLED AND STRUGGLING, THE BIRD WAS OURS.

49. Merlin (Prairie)

Falco columbarius

For anyone involved in rescue and rehabilitation of migratory birds, October is a cornucopia of species. When the rancher described the bird encamped near her winter stack of firewood, she asked if there are albinos among small hawks. "It's just plain washed out as far as color is concerned." Comparing it in size to the American kestrels that frequented the ranch, the woman was puzzled by what she had.

Relating that the hawk-like visitor had been hanging around the ranch house for days, she was concerned about its poor flight ability when attempting to perch atop a fence post or the cord of wood. Through her binoculars, the rancher had noticed the ragged edge of the bird's tail. "Been down a while. Do you think it could be somebody's bird?" she asked. When she called later that afternoon to say she had been able to catch the bird easily, we headed northwest some 46 miles to the ranch.

After meeting the lady and seeing the prairie merlin, we agreed with her that the visitor had probably been forced to land, rest, and seek refuge at her ranch because of the wind, rain, and hailstorm spawned by our unusually warm fall. Having left his Canadian breeding grounds, her autumn guest might have migrated through eastern Colorado and New Mexico. Once inside western Texas, the falcon was fortunate to encounter a host who realized he needed help.

Placing the merlin on his back with his head covered to calm him, we extended the pale, blueish-gray, long pointed wings. Feeling no obvious fractures, we noticed the white throat and creamy white underparts streaked with brown. Its tapered gray tail, barred with black, was tipped with white. As the ranch owner and we compared the merlin to a kestrel, she realized that her bird was slightly larger, but certainly not as colorful. Obvious was the lack of the distinctive facial stripe that augments a kestrel's attire.

Feeling the merlin may have suffered soft-tissue injuries or bruising from the hail, we decided his journey to Mexico and even South America would have a detour. Until the falcon could resume his fast, powerful flight, he would recuperate at the Lubbock wildlife center.

"Must be what my father used to call a pigeon hawk," commented the rancher as we traded information regarding her find. Her dad had watched the seasonal falcons overtake and easily snatch, with their taloned feet, small birds out of the air.

As we described how these streamlined flyers, with their superb eyesight, spot their prey from above, we added that the prairie merlins partially fold their wings and plunge downward toward their next meal. To our comment, "They may be small in stature, but they're huge in their ferocious attack," she said now she really appreciated even more her father's stories.

"Up close, it's obvious he was not an albino. But from a distance, he looked so pale," was her next observation. Compared to other birds, the merlin had given a first impression of being faded and barely colored. After we had examined the bird, and she had observed the falcon's markings, she understood why she had been mistaken.

In the autumns of the future, the ranch owner would understand why the prairie merlins frequented her land. Her stock ponds would provide for small water birds, while her feeders attracted blackbirds and sparrows. The pastures filled with doves would also offer mice, lizards, small snakes, and insects to fuel the merlins' journey southward. Her family had long accepted nature's ability to overproduce some species as food for others, and this prairie merlin had reminded her of its place in the environment.

50. SHORT-EARED OWL

Asio flammeus

Anticipating the "night of nights," her children quickly climbed inside the pickup with their dad. Since he had promised this year's Halloween would be held at their home on the outskirts of Stanton, a trip to the city for decorations the day before was essential. "Can we go ahead and decorate this evening?" asked the oldest. "Don't see why not," was his reply.

The sound of gravel being crunched in the driveway alerted his wife they had returned. With some daylight left, they had time, before dinner was ready, to set out their ghostly treasures. Since everyone was outside, she could get the table set and read the front page of the paper. When she looked at her watch, she realized they were taking longer than usual. "Might as well wash a few pans," she thought as she approached the sink. Glancing out the window at the backyard, she couldn't recall having a stump near the woodpile. After it blinked, she realized what it was.

As her son, daughter, and husband entered the living room, she congratulated them on decorating the entire yard. Not knowing what she meant, their father looked puzzled. "What do you mean?" he asked. Motioning for them to follow her, she went to the kitchen window.

"Where'd you get that owl? It looks almost real," she questioned as she looked over her glasses at her husband. He knew how she watched every penny. "Mom, honest, we didn't buy any owl," said her daughter as she tried to defend her father. Turning back to the window, they stared at the motionless stump. "Are you sure that's an owl?" asked her son. He made up his own mind when the bird suddenly opened its wings.

Determined to get to the bottom of their prank, the woman hurried out the back door and walked toward "another unnecessary expense." Hearing her approach before opening its eyes, the flat-faced owl sidled slowly to the end of the stacked wood. From the back porch, her children and husband could hear her gasp and cry, "Oh, my goodness!"

When the phone rang, the caller reminded me that she had brought us an owl several years ago. The bird in her backyard didn't look like anything they'd ever seen. Realizing that it had a problem, she and her husband managed to place a blanket over the owl. Carefully, they lowered it into a cardboard box. Willing to drive to Big Spring, they delivered their Halloween extra.

Upon seeing the bird, we knew we had never handled a short-eared owl. No wonder the couple thought it was a stump. Nature had provided this bird of prairies, sand dunes, and open country with mottled feathers that resemble tree bark covered with lichen. By day, its brownish orange wings would contrast with the warm buff of its breast. Hidden were its horns or ear tufts. Even in flight, and rarely when perched, were these special feathers in view.

Before they left, we mentioned that fall migration had brought their visitor. Known to hunt at dusk and dawn, the owls might also be seen sitting on fence posts watching for prey during late afternoon. The fact that the short-eared would hunt during daylight set it apart from other owls. Since the specie nested and even slept on the ground, their bird was essentially a ground owl.

After examining the owl's wings, we planned a Halloween visit to the South Plains rehab center in Lubbock. Between the elbow and wrist of the right wing was a telltale bump. Whether the

broken bone was mendable was of concern. For the bird not to be able to circle, then glide close to the ground would be a loss, especially in the hunting of rodents and insects. Its skill at using the wind and gracefully sailing over grasslands was threatened.

At the wildlife center, the manager determined the radius was broken. After the bone was wired, the owl was expected to recover after a lengthy stay. In the future, it could use its silent wings to dive and drop upon its unsuspecting prey. With the ability to clap its wings in flight, the short-eared owl once again would, on the downward stroke of its wings, strike them together rapidly beneath its body. Sounding like a flag fluttering in the breeze, perhaps it would also be applauding those who had helped in its doing so.

51. Harris's Hawk

Parabuteo unicinctus

When the man arrived at the telephone pole, the lineman had already placed a large bird nest on the ground. "At least this one wasn't a complete loss," said the coworker. Then he explained that on the west side of their district it had rained longer and harder. The big nest they had been watching became so saturated it caused a ground. Both pole and nest were set on fire. "What a night!" he added before going on to the next incident.

As the man looked down at the large hawk lying in the grass, he already knew she had been electrocuted. His friend and fellow nest-watcher had notified him in case he wanted to take the babies and try to save them.

Fortunately, the worst part of the storm had veered to the northeast. The outer fringes, however, had produced enough rain to soak the youngsters. Acting quickly to dry their emerging feathers, he wrapped them in old rags and drove home. Finally dry and warm, the two nestlings slept.

Knowing the birds were meat-eaters, his wife made a quick trip to the grocery store. Her decision to buy stew meat was well-received by the hungry hawks. Soon they were strong and active enough to be placed outside in the children's play-fort that her husband had built. With four surrounding wooden walls, the structure allowed the birds room to exercise and flap their wings.

When the children came home from school each day, they enjoyed feeding the growing hawks their daily ration of stew meat. Soon, the older bird learned that by using its wings, it could stair-step its way to the top. Able to see beyond the walls, the hawk could watch not only its sibling below, but also the countryside beyond his backyard home. It wasn't long until it decided to investigate this new world. With an upward leap and flapping of wings, the fledgling discovered early flight. When hunger persuaded it to return to the fort, it joined the younger hawk in accepting the family's generous meal.

As muscle tone increased, the hawk was soon perched in nearby mesquites. Throughout the day, it was seen flying and supposedly hunting. Its younger sibling finally joined it and tried to mimic its actions. Although the man and his wife assumed the hawks had released themselves to the wild, they continued to offer stew meat.

Gradually, the older hawk sometimes refrained from coming back to feed. However, the younger one came more often, but seemed to be learning to hunt. When the woman noticed one day that it was back but on the ground, she hurried outside. Lying on the ground, the fledgling did not accept her offer of stew meat. Unable to stand, it was obviously very weak.

When the family arrived with the Harris's hawk, fear was evident on their faces. "How long have you had this bird?" was my first question, followed by "What have you been feeding it?" For two months, the hawks had been fed nothing but stew meat. Stressing that the hawks' only knowledge of what they needed to eat looked like raw beef, I stated they did not know they should be seeking rabbits, mice, rats, and even small birds. They had never learned how to hunt and kill their natural food. Apparently, the older hawk may have seen other Harris's hawks in the region and been able to watch them kill their prey. The younger had not had this opportunity.

The fate of the older bird was also in question. When asked what to do about the one they thought had been successful, I suggested they trap mice and hunt rabbits, and provide that source of food if the older bird came back. That way it would learn what it needed to hunt.

As for the younger one, there was no body fat on the sides of the breastbone. So thin it could not stand or eat, it was slowly starving to death. Assuring the family that we would do everything possible to save the hawk, I promised to keep in touch.

"Do you think you can save it?" was Art's question when he felt the bird's chest. Handing him the hawk to hold while I tube-fed it, I answered, "We're going to try!"

Minced mice required force-feeding, since the Harris's didn't have the strength to stand and tear its food. When we discovered that it was apparently digesting the baby mice, we were encouraged. Three days later, after numerous feedings, the hawk stood.

At the South Plains wildlife center, volunteers maintained a close watch on the hawk, and called frequently about its progress. Even when it started eating on its own, we all knew it would be a lengthy recovery. With strength and energy increasing, the bird grew restless in its carrier. Moved to a mew in the barn for exercise, the hawk was eager to attain the first perch. Soon it had mastered the highest one. With little human exposure except for the placing of mice inside the mew, the raptor started exhibiting the typical mean and aggressive attitude of a bird of prey.

Finally, the Harris's hawk was ready for the flight cage. After demonstrating an ability to hunt, kill live prey and fly effortlessly, it was ready for release.

Since the hawk belonged to a social and familial specie, it should be released in an area with other Harris's hawks. Calling the game warden from Monahans, I was confident that he knew where groups could be located, since fall migration had begun. Where Crane, Ward, and Ector county lines meet, he knew of an isolated ranch, accessible only by four-wheeled-drive, with no hunting. The day before I called, he had seen Harris's hawks at one of three ponds. These watering areas, spaced in a triangle, were each within a mile of the other. Since wildlife come to water, the Harris's could easily find prey and be with its own specie.

At one of the ponds, the hawk burst from its carrier. Having spent two months at the wildlife center, it was ready for freedom. Flying to a mesquite, the Harris's hawk turned to face the game warden and calmly fluffed its feathers. That evening, the officer called to say, "It's back where it belongs."

52. Peregrine Falcon

Falco peregrinus

WHAT I THOUGHT WAS MY ONE and only chance to handle such a bird occurred nearly ten years ago. Found in open country under a scrubby bush, the raptor became an educational bird for the Lubbock wildlife center because of his wing injury.

When his death was announced four years later, I was saddened by the loss of such a noble creature.

In late August, a call from the Andrews vet clinic alerted us to another. As we drove northwest, we could hardly believe our good fortune.

DELIVERING IT TO
THE WILDLIFE
CENTER, WE
WATCHED THE
EXAMINATION AND
WERE RELIEVED
THAT THE BIRD
WAS THOUGHT TO
BE A PROSPECT FOR
FUTURE RELEASE.

Opening the box and softly muttering "Oh, my God" to myself, I had startled the veterinary attendant who was standing nearby. "Is something wrong?" she inquired. When I told her that in 33 years it would be only the second time for us to handle this specie, her eyes grew large and her respect for the bird was genuine.

Emaciated and extremely thin, the bird of prey had no broken bones. During migration and with extreme expenditures of energy, any avian specie, after enduring hunger due to lack of hunting prowess, could become depleted of body fat. I noticed that the falcon's eye motion was unusual.

After bringing the bird home, we thawed a dove that had been hit by a car months earlier. Two hours later, we checked on the raptor to see if it had eaten; only the dove's skeleton remained. When I relayed this information to the South Plains center, they were elated.

The next morning I noticed the same strange eye movement I had seen the day before, but assumed it could be caused by the results of the bird's arduous journey. Delivering it to the wildlife center, we watched the examination and were relieved that the bird was thought to be a prospect for future release. While there, I noticed the eye movement again. Later that day, volunteer Gail Barnes called to say she saw the same involuntary glance that she, too, had seen earlier. An examination by a veterinarian confirmed our feelings that the bird had a future in the sky. She added that another dove had been placed with the raptor. Again, it had dined readily.

When the phone rang the following day, Gail said, "The peregrine falcon died." Neither of us could understand what had happened. Readily eating twice, the bird had been eager to tear its prey, and could digest its food.

My numbness clouded my thinking and I promised to call back. Before we hung up, Gail added, "We had a peregrine falcon turned in today from Wofford, which is close to Lubbock." My response was, "Keep an eye on it."

Since the falcon we had delivered was still on the "threatened list," I asked that it be tested for any toxins. Fortunately, one of only three avian toxicologists in the United States happened to be at Texas Tech. Willing to perform the analysis to determine the cause of death, Dr. Mike Hooper said it would be a while before we heard anything.

Although the wait for news was agonizing, we were all encouraged by the Wofford falcon. A hole torn in one of its wings had prevented the bird from flying. After finding no broken bones, Larry Farley, D.V.M., delicately sutured the wound. Uncertain if the peregrine would ever fly again, he felt its recovery and rehabilitation held the answer.

After weeks of waiting, the call finally came. Toxic lead in the liver, probably from undrained desert basins called playa lakes, contributed to the death of the falcon from Andrews. When I called the game warden, who had turned it over to the vet clinic, he said he was not surprised:

"You can't imagine the amount of lead that falls into the playas during dove season." Since peregrines prey on the birds coming to the playas for water, it was plausible that they would ingest lead from water birds and the doves hit by only a few of the sprays of ammunition. At least the analysis would alert U. S. Fish & Wildlife Service of the potential danger to the peregrines, which had once been labeled "endangered specie."

During this time, thoughts of what "might-have-been" persisted. Helpful were the weekly reports concerning the progress of the remaining peregrine. After a lengthy conversation in which Gail related how the Wofford falcon was flying effortlessly in the flight cage, she ended her story with the question, "Would you like to release the peregrine? It is more than ready."

Our excitement over giving the falcon its freedom was overwhelming. Handling the bird before release was not considered because to chance an accident caused by the bird's eagerness to be free was risky.

With the peregrine in a cardboard carrier and knowing the corridor that the species uses during fall migration, we headed south of Stanton the last of September. As the SUV was buffeted by thirty-five-mile-an-hour winds, we found an isolated rise that would provide an upward direction for the gusts to turn into rising currents of warm air. A wide dirt road surrounded by low scrubs could be the bird's taxiway.

Before we were able to get out of the vehicle, a turkey vulture suddenly rose from about thirty feet away. With the winds assisting it in flight, we felt we had the right spot. As I carried the container up the road away from the SUV, Art positioned himself for a chance at photographing the peregrine. We were ready for everything we expected to happen. The falcon thought otherwise.

A second after I opened the container, the bird was motionless. Quickly moving its head to survey its surroundings, it purposely slammed its right side into the cardboard to move the carrier in the direction of the wind. With its strong legs and feet, it lunged upward into the gale. Two powerful, downward strokes of its wings sent it forward and straight toward Art. Not expecting the bird to fly directly at him, he ducked and turned as the falcon flew over him and rose above the scrubs. With wings extended, it circled over the two of us as it continued to lift effortlessly on the rising thermal. "It sensed the wind, it sensed the wind!" I yelled to Art, who could barely hear me because of the noise from the gusts. When Art came close enough to hear what I was yelling, then he, too, realized that the peregrine falcon had momentarily waited until it was sure of the direction of the wind.

Using the powerful lift of its wings and the wind, it gained elevation rapidly. Amazed at how quickly it was ascending and how little effort was used, we realized why the species is so respected. Continuing its upward climb, it became smaller and smaller. Soon it would be so high it would disappear.

"It has company!" I exclaimed when another silhouette joined our bird. Together they enjoyed their merry-go-round in the sky. Then Art shouted, "There's another one!" Together, we stood and watched the two seasoned falcons accept our newly released. Only other falcons would be soaring at those elevations.

Knowing the Wofford bird had company on its long journey to the south was comforting. The silhouettes became tiny dots and finally disappeared in the clear sky. The skillful veterinarian and the volunteers had given back to nature one of its fastest creatures. Unable to speak from emotion, we stood silently grateful for the opportunity we thought would never come.

53. Common Loon

Gavia immer

Through the entrance, past the circular desk staffed by city employees constantly answering the phone, we followed the officer through the first of many steel doors. The hallways were becoming familiar. Straight ahead, a turn to the left, then right past the tubs, we walked through yet another door, and into the holding area. While reaching this part of the Midland Animal Control facility, we appreciated the absence of odors. A daily effort was evident in the cleanliness of the place. A monotony of tile walls, concrete floors, and holding cages gave the reality of their work a stark and unforgettable presence.

The quiet, isolated area where birds were kept was appreciated. Through the barred door of the steel container, we could easily see the large water bird resting on its belly with legs and feet splayed. Several weeks before, we had answered a request to pick up a hawk and a falcon. Instead, we had discovered an osprey and a whippoorwill. Incorrect identification of birds was common among not only animal control officers, but the public as well. Of greater importance was our response in retrieving whatever they had rescued. Briefly explaining

the diet and behavior of a bird would lend to more knowledge in the future. We were grateful to be able to identify and obtain the necessary veterinary and rehabilitative care for any migratory birds they had.

Uneasily turning its head to glance backward through the bars, the common loon could not readily turn its heavy body to confront us. Since the bird had been placed headfirst inside the structure, its removal was easier than if we had to confront the jabs from its long, sharp gray bill.

With my hands firmly pressing its wings against its body, I lifted the eight-to-nine pound loon out of its temporary prison. Immediately, its legs that are located at the back of its body began to pedal madly as if on an imaginary bicycle. Round and round its big feet churned the air. "We won't need the bathtub for this one," Art sighed with relief. The loon had proven its ability to ply the waters of any inland lake or deep reservoir.

Suddenly, from the inner depths of the loon's body came a cry of absolute wildness. Guttural, melodic, that moment of the bird's mournful sound caused shivers in both of us as we realized we had heard the voice of a bird

that loves the solitude of northern lakes. The room, with its harsh floor and walls, had amplified our experience.

"Where did you find it?" was my question after carefully inserting the bird inside and onto thick bedding in our carrier. The answer was not surprising, "The parking lot of a Baptist church." Explaining that during migration, loons often mistake the late afternoon sheen of asphalt for what they think is the surface of a body of water, we added that without the adequate length of a lake or pond, the birds could never become airborne again. Only through running on top of the water could it obtain the forward momentum and airspeed for flight.

As the three of us looked at the loon, I noted the bird's non-breeding winter plumage. For its protection, nature has given it a dull appearance of gray to gray-brown above, while its underparts were white. After thanking the officer for calling us, we headed home and to Comanche Lake. We couldn't help but be excited at another launch.

Approaching the water from the south side, we were eager to watch our charge return to a proper environment. Awkward and stumbling when on land to nest, the loon would become grace personified when reintroduced to its watery world.

Placing it on the surface of the lake, we were mesmerized by its immediate dive beneath the surface. Some forty feet away, it surfaced, shook droplets from its feathers, and scanned the shorelines. Diving and resurfacing again and again, it was finding the contents of the lake to its liking. Finally satisfying itself with enough fish, it chose to stay atop and slowly investigate its new habitat.

What had been heavy in my hands was a buoyant, streamlined swimming wonder. For a bird that needs as much space to land as to take off, the loon now had its place. Its strength and speed on and in the water would easily be matched in the coming days by its strong, rapid sustained flight during the rest of its migration.

As we walked back to the vehicle, we knew our experience with another common loon had been heightened by the loveliness of the sounds the bird had shared in protest of our handling it. That cry was unforgettable.

54. Eared Grebe

Podiceps nigricollis

Covered with dried mud, the pickup followed the dirt road as if from memory. Every bounce from the ruts was familiar to both the man and his vehicle. Since his job required his sojourn into the desolate parts of the county, he enjoyed the solitude and his encounters with nature. Surprised by what lay ahead, the man applied the brakes.

Struggling to rise, a small bird in the center of the road had a light film of caliche covering its feathers. The truck coming toward it had caused the creature to panic. Unable to hide or quickly dive and swim away, the bird was frightened when its quiet rest was interrupted. Even more alarming were the crunch of the boots and the size of the man who approached. It had never encountered such a threatening experience.

Quickly, the large, rough hands surrounded the wiggling creature. Taken to the pickup, the bird was wrapped in a towel for the trip to town.

Telling me he thought it might be a water bird, R. C. gently handed over his squirming package. Its short, slender pointed bill was sticking through the terry cloth. Protruding from the other end of the towel were the bird's legs and partially webbed, lobed toes.

"It's a grebe," was my answer to the puzzled look on his face.

When I asked him if he had found it on a paved surface, R. C. shook his head and replied, "No. The middle of a caliche road." Like loons, grebes sometimes mistake the sheen of asphalt for water. Too late they learn that their landing site has made it impossible for them to become airborne again.

We both wondered why a bird that runs on the surface of a lake or pond would decide to land in an area that had no bodies of water. "Maybe it was just exhaustion," was my only thought.

If the little grebe were unhurt and capable of swimming, it would be ready for release. Showing R. C. that the bird's legs were at the back of its body rather than in the middle, I explained that we would place the grebe in the bathtub filled with water. Insuring us that its feet and legs worked properly, the bird would be set free as soon as we could get to a lake. "You've made my day," was part of my thanking him for rescuing the grebe.

In the bathtub, the drabness of its winter plumage was offset by its scarlet eyes. The soft, thick feathers on the upper chest gave the buxom swimmer a more than ample appearance. Dark gray to black above, and white to gray below, the American eared grebe enjoyed paddling the length of the tub. The whitish patch back of each ear helped in our identification.

Convinced of its ability to swim and run, we headed to Comanche Lake. Lifting the grebe from the carrier, I could feel the eagerness of the bird to return to water. After placing it on the water, we watched it immediately dive out of sight. Having swum a short distance, it reappeared. Pleased with its surroundings, the grebe leapt into the air and plunged straight down with closed wings. Almost as quickly as it dove, it resurfaced, only to do it again. While it might have been clumsy on land, it was energized by its precision diving, underwater swimming and feeding. In the deep open water, the bird was finding small fish, aquatic insects, and their larvae. Water plants, flies, moths, midges, and its own body feathers would complete its diet.

Freezing weather on northern lakes had forced the eared grebe to migrate. Its unfortunate landing had resulted in another chance on an inland body of water. Rested and well-fed, the bird would in the near future rise quickly out of the water some moonlit night to continue its flight to a winter haven.

55. Green-winged Teal

Anas crecca

Landing on the slow-moving creek, the bird was carried by the current along the shoreline as it searched for food. The bottomland's dense growth of salt-cedar offered wintering waterfowl protection from predators and a quiet restful place devoid of automobiles and hunters.

As it bobbed forward, then under the shallow water, the small bird probed in the mud for aquatic insects, larvae, and worms. Tender bites of water plants were also taken. In early fall, it had availed itself of berries, wild grapes, nuts, and acorns as its migration took it southward. Grainfields had offered residues of corn, wheat, barley, and oats that it found to its liking.

Floating under the highway bridge, the bird and its companions were a striking sight as they readily fed their insatiable appetites. With bodies half-submerged, feet kicking in the air, the birds seemed to appreciate what nature had given them. Just as they had eaten in one accord, they floated further on the creek until, in unison, they lifted in a strong, swift flight to the southeast.

For weeks employees at the water treatment plant had heard random gunfire. Having alerted law enforce-ment, they hoped it would cease. Since some of their work entailed being outside, they were apprehensive of stray bullets.

Attempts to catch the part-time shooter had been unsuccessful. Daily, a game warden hid in the heavy growth that began at the fence line and continued on downstream. His only companion was silence except for the occasional country traffic. Seeing the closely bunched flock of ducks rise suddenly from the creek to the north, the officer appreciated the sight of waterfowl on an otherwise boring day. As the fliers twisted and turned as they approached the roadway, the startling sharp sound of a gun came from just down the road.

"Could you come and pick up an injured bird?" asked the game warden when he called. "I need a positive ID." Saying we'd be right there, I grabbed a field guide on birds. Since a duck had been mentioned, we might need some pictures for reference. In all the years we'd been called out, I had never heard the officer's voice sound so troubled.

The warden's pickup was parked behind an older model coupe. Pressed against the front of the faded vehicle, with his elbows on the hood, head in hands, appeared to be a teenage boy.

As we walked toward the warden, he motioned for us to stop so the young person could not hear our conversation. I commented that the teenager looked like he was going to throw up. "He already has," replied the officer. Approaching an area of the hood near the teen, the warden gently laid the struggling bird on some old rags atop the metal surface. Then he introduced us as the people who work with injured birds. "Tell him what will happen to the duck."

Extending the wings, we both identified it as a green-winged teal. The injured wing was damaged beyond repair. By federal law, we were obligated to have the bird euthanized.

Handing us the duck, the warden escorted the teen to his pickup. Then he returned. "I know his dad. I've known this kid since he was little. My disappointment in what he did is worse than the fines he'll have to pay. On top of that is his dad." Then he walked back to his truck. Driving off with the teenager, the warden left the coupe and us behind.

In its winter plumage, the small, brownish-gray duck I held in my lap had a buff-colored breast spotted with black. Visible, even with its wings closed, were the patches of green, iridescent feathers which contrasted with the surrounding feathers of each wing.

This little teal had been denied his colorful plumage of the next breeding season. Never again would he sport the glossy-green ear patches on each side of his brown head. Nor the white vertical stripes on each side of his breast in front of his wing feathers.

The breeding strut of the male, as it stood up in the water with extended wings, no longer would be enjoyed by this bird on a northern lake. By a single shot, an ancient ritual had been silenced.

56. Northern Pintail

Anas acuta

Even inside the house, she heard what sounded like the backfire of a car. "Must be Tony's," she thought as she continued her housework. "That boy is either gunning the engine in that old wreck or the engine's sputtering," she thought. Hope for a quiet neighbor died quickly when his family bought the house next door.

Later in the afternoon, she glanced out the front window to see if the school-age children were walking home. She could set her watch by their daily routine.

Movement in the leaves underneath her live oak tree caught her attention.

Appearance-wise, the slender long-necked bird looked like a skinny duck. Slipping into a heavy sweater, she headed toward the front door.

As she approached the bird, it tried to fly. Coming straight off the ground with a burst of energy, it fell back to the yard as soon as it tried to flap its wings. Realizing its situation, she slowly backed away so as not to frighten the bird anymore.

"It has to be a duck," said the concerned woman on the phone. "I've never seen one like this. It's long and thin. So are its neck and tail," she continued. Not knowing what to anticipate, I headed for the southwest side of town.

Meeting me at the driveway, the woman had decided to stay in her yard until I arrived. She could prevent anyone from getting too close to the bird.

Upon seeing the duck, I could appreciate her excitement in describing the Northern pintail as elegant and beautiful. A rich brown adorned the drake's slim head and upper neck. His white breast, in wrapping around to the sides, had tapered upward to form a white neck stripe that ended in a point on either side. With brown-gray back and sides, the duck had a white patch at the rear of his flanks. Gracing his back were long, narrow feathers. Prominent were two long, pointed, middle tail feathers that extended beyond the brown-gray tail.

With a net on a long pole, I was able to catch the duck before he exploded from the ground again. As sleek as he was, the bird had a healthy resistance to being captured. Removing the net, I held him against a soft cushion of leaves as I extended each narrow, pointed wing. Both the woman and I could hardly contain our enthusiasm when we saw the iridescent patch of green and bronze displayed on each wing.

The displaced feathers on the left wing, however, were of concern. Laying the duck on his back and covering his head with a towel, I could readily see the small droplets of dried blood that had seeped from what appeared to be a gunshot wound. Apparent to the touch was an irregular bump on one of the wing bones. "Can it be fixed?" asked the woman as I placed the pintail in a carrier. Telling her I would have to take him to a rehabilitation center, I promised to let her know the outcome.

Verifying that the Northern pintail had been shot, the wildlife center volunteer offered some optimism. After the setting of the wing, the duck would spend many weeks before anyone would know if the knitting of the bone had been successful. After he spent considerable time in exercising his wing, we would learn if he were capable of flight. If not, a conservation lake was available for the bird to become a permanent resident.

In rethinking the events that led to his capture, the woman and I felt the pintail had probably rested with others on our city lake that was nearby. Since it was early February, I told her I thought the drake had already started migrating the previous month. Headed toward his nesting grounds, it would be April or May before he reached the Alaskan tundra.

Puzzling to us was how anyone could hit such a fast-moving bird. When I asked some duck hunters, their answer came readily. The pintails bunch together when taking flight and are easily shot. Once the duck was down, they felt it had walked into her yard to seek refuge.

With the pintail's freedom questionable, the woman and I were satisfied that he was receiving the best of care. Although he might never experience another season of courtship, we had been privileged to see and touch the luxurious feathers of what must be nature's ultimate tuxedo.

57. Turkey Vulture — "Old Man"

Cathartes aura

As the cool north breeze hurled bits of paper and dust toward him, the old fellow continued his aimless search for anything to sustain him. Occasionally he found some of his daily ration carelessly left among the trash. Soiled and greasy from his surroundings, he was continuously hungry and growing thinner. Overtime, his feet had become sore from walking over the crushed glass and debris. Alone, he didn't want to be there, but could find no way out.

Having spotted a uniformed employee, he tried not to be noticed. The equipment operator had seen the guy before, but every time someone tried to approach, the old-timer awkwardly ran to keep his distance.

Determined to get him some help, the operator decided one morning to get closer. Taking a chance, the employee used a personal vehicle and decided to chase the guy until confronting him. It took some time, turning here and there, but through maneuverability and determination, the operator cornered the derelict. Chasing him on foot finally caused the old fellow to stop and gasp for air. Unable to run anymore, the oldster was caught by two hands that were not going to let go.

Placed in a holding area, the old fellow stood with his head down. Locked up like a vagrant, he appeared hopeless and disoriented. He was watched by attendants as they processed others.

Then, over several days, he encountered numerous baths and free feeds. Placed with two others in a larger, more comfortable lodging, he was readily accepted by his roommates. He rested and improved.

When asked to repeat the story of the greasy turkey vulture from a landfill, I could hear an occasional chuckle from Gail Barnes, manager of the wildlife center in Lubbock. Two days before, we had been called to an animal control facility in a large metropolitan area. Their officer had retrieved the bird from a concerned employee at the dump. Since we had often taken various species from their care, we were asked if we wanted the vulture.

Until we removed the raptor from its cage, we had been told only it could not fly. Once we had examined it, we knew why. The vulture was a greasy, gritty, matted bundle of feathers. Its wings, tail, and body were heavily laden with an oily substance. The weight of the coating on its once blackish-brown feathers would prevent any flight.

Fortunately for us, the bird had been placed headfirst in the container. At least with his head pointed away from me, if he decided to disgorge the contents of his crop or stomach in a defensive gesture, only the floor would suffer.

"The greasy mess is not coming off the way it should," was Gail's comment when she described the numerous baths in Blue Dawn. Since she thought it might have a petroleum base, we countered by saying we did not think it could be oil field-related. First, it did not have the odor. In addition, even though it was a thin coating, it remained oily to the touch. The bird would probably have died if it had been a petroleum product.

It was obvious that the vulture had not flown into the fenced landfill in that condition. Whatever was on its feathers was acquired at the site. We all agreed that the bird would have to remain at the center until having a complete molt, which would begin in spring and could continue through summer and into early fall.

"By the way, we have a name for your vulture," Gail offered. "Did you notice all of the warts around its eyes? Usually you see that in the elderly, even people," she added. "We're going to call him 'Old Man.' He's getting along with the other two so well, he may not want to leave."

Wanting to know more about the landfill, I called several residents of that city and county. Their stories were too similar to ignore. Cooking oils and grease from restaurants were being discharged into two open pits. Wildlife could easily slide into the pits on the slippery liners, or mistake them for water from the air.

With its keen sense of smell, the turkey vulture had probably been attracted to the landfill during its migratory journey. Old Man would not have killed animals, but would have sought out the dead. Even decaying carcasses, if not buried deeply, would have emitted the aroma of a possible meal. How it had accumulated such a greasy coating that attracted dust and windblown particles, only the large soaring bird knew.

The outcome of the pits would be dictated by governmental agencies. Through Old Man's unsightly appearance, an alarm had been sounded.

58. Great Horned Owl

Bubo virginianus

Two weeks prior to the telephone call, we had been with Midge and Woody Erskine at their Eos Wildlife Sanctuary in Midland. Although we had rescued and transported several birds of prey, this would be our first time to force-feed one of the larger birds. Excited and apprehensive at the same time, we looked forward to learning more.

Grabbing and holding a struggling raptor, Midge then encouraged me to open its beak and give it small chunks of rabbit, while Art watched the effort. After closely following her verbal directions, my hands were nearly on the bird's beak when her husband, Woody, cautioned, "Always remember, those birds can bite off your finger or thumb. Fortunately, they don't know that," he added as he left the room.

Hoping no one could hear how loud my heart was beating and checking to make sure my hands weren't shaking, I proceeded to pry open the massive beak. It was quite an introduction to the tremendous force the bird could exert on any prey. As the lesson progressed, we also were instructed in how to capture the bird by its legs. Impressive were the feet and talons. The slightest misstep in handling meant a possible "footing" by the bird.

Like an "X," each foot had two talons forward, two behind. The crushing power of its feet enabled it to squeeze and hold on to its catch. Able to lift large prey, some of which were heavier than the bird, made it an aggressive and proficient hunter.

Our previous experiences with this type of bird had been easy in comparison. A large blanket or old coat thrown over the bird had enabled us to press its wings against its body. With a quick uplifting movement, we had quickly put the raptor in a cardboard box and secured the top. Knowing we would not always have that easy a capture, we felt it imperative to know more about handling difficult situations.

About to use the knowledge we had previously gained, we hurried to answer the call from Big Spring Animal Control. They had a large raptor that could not fly. Without the luxury of additional space for birds, the officer requested that we remove it from a long, narrow cage in the back of one of their pickups as soon as possible.

As we entered the parking area of the city's "pound," we realized its location near Beal's Creek and the railroad tracks had been accurately described by citizens wanting a better locale. Even though the buildings offered temporary shelter, the personnel seemed genuinely concerned about their charges. No one could truly appreciate how limited they were in resources during the '70s.

When the officer lowered the tailgate, we knew this capture was going to be a challenge. Since the cage occupied the length of the truck bed, I would have to enter and exit by crawling the distance on my knees. There would be little room to spare. At the other end, pressed against the back of the cage, was a frightened, very angry adult great horned owl.

Expressing his concern for my safety, Art asked, "Are you sure you want to do this?" If we turned the cage on end, the bird might hold onto the sides with its talons, or if it did plummet downward, a wing could be damaged further. Only one choice remained.

As we started to unload what we thought we might need for this attempt, Art noticed a bright orange towel among our gear. Given to him by his best man shortly after our wedding, he had never used the thick, oversized beach towel. Since Tony couldn't find the burnt orange of their university days, he had selected what he consid-

ered close in color. My only thought had been that it would glow in the dark.

We readily ruled out a pole net, since the cage was too narrow for its use. Deciding on my leather gardening gloves and the orange towel, I asked Art to walk slowly beside the truck about a foot ahead. Holding the towel at the top two corners inside the cage, I would not be able to judge what the owl was doing. If the bird could see only the fabric approaching, rather than me, it might lessen its fear. Hopefully, my approach would keep it at the back of the cage. Pressing the owl against that area could assist in its capture.

As the officer opened the cage door, the owl began harsh popping sounds as it clicked its beak. The warning was accompanied by its swaying from side to side while it tried to look as large as possible. When I was about a foot and a half from the end of the cage, the owl struck blindly at the towel with its feet.

When one foot's talons became caught in the thick terry cloth to my right, I reached for the leg I knew was on the other side, while holding the rest of the towel with my left hand and elbow. The bird's other leg and foot hit the lower part of the towel about an inch from my left knee. Grabbing at that area and missing with my left hand, I met his taloned foot as it came forward again. Due to the thickness of the towel in addition to the leather glove, the great horned's

talons did not penetrate enough to grab my fingers.

Quickly, while the owl tried to untangle its foot from the towel, I reached higher and secured the remaining leg. Recalling the advice from two weeks before, I could hear Midge saying, "Control the feet and you control the bird." How true that was!

Securing both legs with my right hand, I quickly used my left hand to wrap the remaining part of the bulky towel around the wiggling, popping owl. My retreat from this confinement was slow as the owl continued to fight the orange covering.

As we unwrapped the great horned, I suddenly realized we had an audience. Another officer and several city employees from another department had come to watch the show. With

widely-spaced ear tufts on its large head, the owl sported a barred chest with mottled shades of brown. Its white throat and big yellow eyes were a striking contrast. Art told the men, considering its size, he thought it was a female and where we would be taking it.

Upon hearing that the wing in question had a hairline fracture that was mendable, we were ecstatic. The great horned owl could be released in the future. With a growing appreciation of the bird's natural defenses came the realization that we would be gaining knowledge from every rescued bird. And on future challenges, the bright orange towel would become a mainstay as it slowly faded and acquired memorable holes.

59. Northern Shovelers

Anas clypeata

THE WEATHER HAD BEEN UNSEASONABLY warm for February. Having had the day off, the game warden enjoyed starting his yearly garden. About three o'clock, he decided to check his answering machine. With no calls, he took the opportunity to work outside several more hours. Closing the back door, he was several feet from the house when the recorder took the message.

Proud of what he had accomplished, the officer glanced at clouds building in the distance. "Finished just in time," he thought, as he quit for the day.

145

As the thunderheads had grown in size, a desolate area south of town offered the only shimmering surface for a small number of migrating birds. As they instinctively descended toward a place to weather out the slow-moving storm, the first drops of rain splattered on the dusty ground surrounding a pond.

The foursome, while resting from their flight, would strain water and mud through the projections along the sides of their spatula-like bills. Their surface feeding would include small fish, water insects, snails, and aquatic worms. The birds would also seek out buds and young shoots of water plants. In his mating plumage, the drake was noticeably more colorful than the three smaller females. As the birds landed, the white embellishment on the underside of their wings was evident in both sexes. Once on the surface, the drake's iridescent dark green head, white breast, pale blue wing patch, and rusty brown belly and flanks made the grayish-brown females look even more nondescript. Their only colorful attribute was an orangish bill in comparison to his black one.

Having watched their landing while reading a gauge on a nearby vessel, an employee called for his supervisor. Not getting an answer, the man knew that no matter what he did, he'd be in trouble. After trying to think of all the consequences, he made another call. Time after time, he reached an answering machine. The message he left was finally answered.

"When did this happen?" asked the game warden after reaching the caller. "Shortly after three," was the reply. Knowing he would need help, the officer quickly called two other wardens to assist. Even though he was dirty and sweaty from his day's gardening, he quickly changed into his uniform. It wouldn't stay clean long, he thought, as he started out in pouring rain.

Some fifteen miles south, he turned to the east. Having to drive slower due to the deluge, he could barely see the road in spite of having his windshield wipers on high. Eight miles further, he parked and waited for the other wardens to arrive.

When the officers entered the pond area, standing with the employee who had called were representatives of his company. Using their dip nets, the wardens removed four ducks from the surface of a pit. With one officer remaining at the facility, the other two rushed the oil-soaked ducks to town.

"Can you identify some birds for us?" came the plea from the game warden. Since we had just started watching the ten o'clock news, I invited him to come to our home. Then he told me he was parked outside in the driveway. As he and the other officer came toward the porch with a cardboard box, I could smell a distinct aroma. "We're not coming inside. We'd just get oil all over the place," said his fellow officer.

Since the rain had stopped, we could readily use the porch light and the emerging light of the moon through the clouds. "Shovelers. Northern Shovelers," was all I could say. Two of the ducks had died. The remaining two were in shock and gasping for breath.

After looking at the smaller female that was barely alive, I lifted the drake. Dripping oil and unable to lift his head, he twitched from the spasms wracking his body. Suddenly he was limp. His suffering had ended.

All four ducks had been in the open pit since three o'clock. Even though the wardens had been able to get them out of the oil, they knew, as did we, that the birds would not survive. Absorbed through the skin as well as being swallowed, the crude oil and chemicals would slowly kill the shovelers. To solidify their case, the officers had to have us identify the ducks.

Overcome by the agony of the dying shovelers., none of us could speak. Accustomed to seeing the worst that could be inflicted on wildlife, the two officers shifted from foot to foot while gaining their composure. Telling them there was nothing we could do for the remaining bird, we knew the shovelers would become evidence. To further their case, the men would return to the

pit that night to continue dredging for any other remains.

As the officers turned to leave, I noticed that although their pants were splattered with oil, their shoes were clean. "We threw our boots in the back of the truck," was their parting comment.

Their night was going to be a long one.

Walking back to the house, we noticed oily stains on my slacks, shoes, and the front porch. This seemed incidental compared to the penalties we, and the wardens, thought the company would have to pay. Recent legislation stated that open pits were to be covered to prevent such an incident. Game wardens would gain assistance in enforcement of such laws. Industry was being held accountable.

Within a week, we learned differently. Instead of the expected monetary punishment, an arrangement was construed between a governmental department and the offender. The total value of the shovelers was lowered to the equivalent of being fined for fishing without a license.

In the eighteen years since, industry has improved. Violations and the death of birds still occur, but to a lesser degree. The laws are still in effect, but their interpretation varies. When the story of that night was written by an investigative reporter for the Austin American-Statesman, a controversy

began over enforcement of environmental laws. With the death of the northern shovelers, dialogue had at least begun.

60. Swainson's Hawk – "Toenails"

Buteo swainsoni

AS THE MORNING'S SUNLIGHT WARMED its feathers, the nestling stirred. Kept warm during the night by its mother's body heat, it looked forward to the bits of food she would soon be bringing. Pushing against the leaves and twigs in the bottom of its home, it stretched to lay its head and neck on the side of the nest. In the distance, the flapping of wings grew louder as its parent approached her hungry brood.

Having satisfied their appetites momentarily, the mother bird flew away. If she couldn't capture a ground squirrel or mouse to feed

herself and two offspring, then the large grasshoppers in the area would suffice.

Snuggling against its sibling, the baby slept. When the nest trembled slightly, the nestling thought its parent had returned. As it rose to meet another offering, it was startled when it was surrounded and jerked from the nest. Suddenly, the light of morning disappeared.

Another scorcher was predicted for the first day of August. Using the early morning for our outdoor work, we stopped to have a glass of tea. Having listened to our recorder, Art came back to the table with a worried look on his face. "Bird call. A hawk."

Listening to the machine's message several times, I heard an intermittent noise as the speaker requested help. When I returned the man's call, the familiar sound continued as he described the problem. We left immediately for the south part of town.

After parking in front of the man's home, I heard the call as I stepped from the truck. As we walked toward the backyard, again it came, that desperate cry. Greeting us as we entered the gate, the homeowner stopped working on his home renovation project. He, too, would soon have to seek shade or the coolness of his home.

"It's in the easement. Been crying like that for some time," he noted as he pointed toward some tall, dry grasses on the other side of the fence. Leaving the yard and entering the easement, we walked to the area he had mentioned. Not seeing anything, we looked back toward the homeowner, who added, "Gotta be there somewhere."

Checking every foot of the tall weeds, we finally saw the hawk crouched as low as it could get in among the grasses. Feathered, the young juvenile did not run when I approached it. As I knelt in order to be on its level, the raptor leaned back on its rump, with wings slightly open. Crouching again, the bird was quickly trapped as Art placed our pole net over it. Reaching under the net, I grasped its legs and raised it from its hiding place.

Removing strands of grass from its back and wings, I nodded to Art to spread our old towel on the ground so I could lay the hawk on its back. He knew I would continue to pick bits of dried weeds and stickers from the front of the bird, as well as feel its breastbone to determine body fat.

Once we had positioned the bird, I noticed its feet. "Oh, no!" I sighed loudly. On the other side of the fence, the homeowner asked what was wrong. Tears welling in my eyes, I looked up at the man without speaking. Taking a deep breath, I answered, "Someone has cut off every one of its talons."

Kneeling over the bird, I had never felt such a deep abhorrence and hatred toward any human being. Whoever had done this to the bird had sentenced it to a life of captivity. Apparently, the Swainson's hawk had been taken from its nest for the benefit of someone who could only gain in stature from possessing a bird of prey.

"Did a falconer do that?" asked the man. "No," we answered, "licensed falconers fly and hunt their birds. With no talons, this bird could not catch, grasp, or hold anything." We added that anyone working with wild birds would never subject any raptor to such abuse.

After examining the Swainson's, we told the homeowner the bird would have starved to death if it had not been found. It was weak, with little body fat. Needing food and dependent upon its captor, the young hawk had called in desperation.

Although the bird could exist on insects and mice, it would have been difficult for it to catch anything with its feet. The talons had been clipped back to the stubby end of each toe. Unable to roost because it could not grip a limb, the hawk was essentially a ground bird and in danger from feral animals and night creatures.

Once home, and after supplying the hawk with mice, we knew its continued verbal calling was in response not only to wanting food, but also a way of communicating because it was imprinted on humans. Even after we left its area, the bird would call. If it heard us in the next room, it chanced that a cry would bring more food and us.

Calling the wildlife center in Lubbock, I advised the manager, Gail Barnes, that we had an intermediate juvenile Swainson's hawk. As I started to relate the rescue, my voice broke. My inability to continue was a clue that something was terribly wrong. Patiently, Gail waited. Finally, I told her someone had clipped off all of the bird's talons. She was horrified.

"Will this hawk be able to grow new talons? Also, you won't believe the feathers on its head, back, and wings. This bird looks as if it has been greased. Its feathers are slicked down," I continued. Wondering if the bird had come from a body shop, or some place for car repairs, Gail also thought maybe it was covered with hydraulic fluid. Having already considered this, I told her we felt it was almost like a gel of some kind. There was no odor.

Three days later, we delivered the Swainson's to the wildlife center. Hearing of the bird's plight was bad enough. Seeing it was a shock. "It's worse than I thought," was Gail's comment after looking at the bird's feet. With the promise of a phone call as soon as the veterinarians examined it, we drove home.

"Some good news for you," said Gail. "The talons were clipped when the bird was a nestling. If it had been done later, the hawk would have bled to death." Over time, the talons were going to grow out. The bird could then hold its food while tearing it with its beak. Eventually it would be able to grasp a roost.

Since it could never be released, the center planned to keep it as an educational bird. Telling us it had been talking, or calling, ever since, they were giving the hawk the attention it so desperately needed. The volunteers decided to name the hawk Toenails. Its name would give its handlers many opportunities to repeat his story.

Six months later, the Swainson's still had mottled brown wing feathers and a grayish tail with narrow bands. His cinnamon breast with rounded spots and the streaking on his belly were beginning to change to a buffy white. Already developing was his dull-brown breast band or "bib."

Best of all, Toenails' talons were growing. Although they were uneven and not tapered to a point as in nature, the raptor was roosting, catching and holding his food, and becoming an integral part of the educational program at the center.

MY INABILITY TO CONTINUE WAS A CLUE THAT SOMETHING WAS TERRIBLY WRONG. PATIENTLY, GAIL WAITED. FINALLY, I TOLD HER SOMEONE HAD CLIPPED OFF ALL OF THE BIRD'S TALONS. SHE WAS HORRIFIED.

61. ROCK DOVE

Columba livia

When the windows, house and we shook in unison, the outcome was inevitable. It had to be the Big Spring refinery. Rising dark smoke confirmed our suspicion.

As we drove to an outlook from which to view the fire, we knew the damage would be extensive. Art's thirty-four years in the engineering department had prompted both of us to leave without breakfast, even our coffee, in order to see the effects to "our refinery."

From a hill that gave an uncluttered view of the entire facility, we saw more than the billowing darkness that announced a massive failure. While Art was mentally assessing the different areas involved, I watched for the familiar signs of life.

As the helicopters circled the plant, I finally found the ever-present fluttering I had hoped to see. Pesky as tumbleweeds, the resilient rock doves had not only survived the blast, but were looking for another roosting site.

Between occasional bursts of conversation as we passed the binoculars back and forth, I thought back to the various birds we had handled from the confines of the refinery. Drenched in crude oil, a cattle egret had been the

impetus for our long involvement with avian populations. An open pit had been its fatal attraction.

Our introduction to the American kestrel, commonly known as a sparrow hawk, had been from the fledglings wandering through the alkylation unit. Towers had provided not only an acceptable elevation but also a safe environment for the mother bird and her nestlings. Jumping from the structures during their first attempts at flight, the youngsters had rested on the ground and strayed in spite of their parent's prodding.

Leaving the hillside to grab a quick brunch, we returned to our vantage point. Even with the fires under control, we still wanted to be there. More memories surfaced, especially of the water birds that had mistaken slick, wet slabs of concrete for a pond's surface. Grebes and teals had quickly been referred to us.

When an employee had told us about yet another water bird, he started by saying, "Now, it's not a duck. Not a goose. But it's fat and short." Asking him about color and its beak, he answered, "That bird is dark, dark gray, with a black head. Has a short white beak. It's an old…..uh, old…" "Coot," I

replied. "Yeah, an old coot!"

Found at the stormwater pond, the American coot was on a pipe spanning the catchall. When approached, it went into the water. Refinery personnel had drained the pond to reach the bird. Diving into the oily sludge at the bottom, the coot was a mess, to say the least.

Late one evening, another water bird had needed attention. Found with oil on its feathers, the shift crew had taken the duck to a kitchen area in the maintenance barn. Bathing the bird numerous times, they dried it as much as they could with a stack of rags. After heating the oven to a low temperature, they placed a non-flammable material on the opened door. On top of that the duck was placed so her feathers could dry completely. By the time we arrived, the female had an audience of men on their break. Enjoying the warmth, she seemed perfectly contented to spend the night.

After having run some errands, we returned once again to the hill. Through the binoculars, the flight of the rock doves indicated that although temporarily homeless, they would be persistent in their intent to reside within the refinery. While some birds sought lofty abodes, others water, the feral pigeons were descendants of the first birds to be domesticated around 4500 B.C. In the early 1600s, their ancestors had been introduced to this country. They felt empowered.

With food readily available from the grains hauled by passing trains, and seeds from surrounding fields, the pigeons sustained their existence and population by the seemingly endless number of open pipe supports for nesting. When a plant manager had asked me how to go about relocating the birds, any recommendation I offered came with a large price tag.

Closing every pipe or metal barrier for a plant that size presented a prohibitive cost. Poisons were eliminated because hawks and owls would readily take available prey.

Later that evening, thought was given to the refinery and its wildlife. Over the years, pits had been netted or covered, non-functioning towers removed, and the plant had become cleaner and safer. Ironically, it seemed that out of bad came good. Whether through planned improvements or untimely explosions, the refinery grew in safety and production.

Retirement offered generations of men and women a rest, while others accepted the challenges. Despite the noise and aromas, birds were always there. As long as there were pipes to perch on, towers, available food, and water, feathered friends would co-exist. The health of the refinery seemed to be reflected in the birds that persisted in calling it home.

62. White-faced Ibis

Plegadis chihi

Grabbing his waders and hat, the game warden neared the office door. "Guy says he has a stork," were his parting words to the secretary as he started a long drive to the ranch. Since he knew the location of the prairie pothole, he had told the rancher to meet him there.

Once he turned onto the dirt road, a trail of dust followed him for miles. Topping over the last hill, he saw what he considered an old buffalo wallow from the past. A year of abundant rains had kept the depression filled with life-giving water. The boot-sucking muds would eventually turn to dust again if the promises of drought held true.

Parked under the scattered shade of an old mesquite was the rancher's pickup. As the officer pulled up beside it, the rancher pointed toward the other end of the pond.

Reaching for his binoculars as he stepped to the ground, the warden asked the man if he had seen it fly. "It just wades and pokes that long beak down in the water to the mud," was his answer. "When I approached it last week, it stayed far enough ahead that I guess it felt safe. Frankly, I don't think it can fly."

Using the glasses, the officer confirmed that this migrant was not a stork. Telling the rancher that while the long bill and large body would make him think so, what he had was an ibis.

At a distance, the large bird appeared dark-colored. Through the binoculars, both men could appreciate the beauty of its breeding plumage. While its upper parts were glossed with iridescent purple, green, and bronze feathers, the underparts were a rich chestnut brown. Its long, down-curved bill had a pointed tip.

Long-necked and long-legged, the ibis was a wading bird. Often seen in the shallow fresh waters of inland ponds and lakes of the Southwest, it also was a winter resident of coastal marshes.

Deciding to split up and approach the ibis from two directions, the men had a long walk. As each neared the other end of the pond, the bird hesitated, before walking further into the shallow water. Following closely, the warden signaled the rancher to wait.

Each time the ibis moved his slightly webbed, long-toed feet forward, the officer followed at the same pace. When the bird stopped, so did he. Finally, the warden decided to test the bird. As quickly as he could, he waded closer to the ibis. Startled, it tried to fly.

The rancher had been correct. Although the bird held its wings equally to its body, its attempt to become airborne was futile. In the confused moment of flapping its wings but not elevating, the warden was able to place his pole net over the ibis.

Pinning the bird to the water, the warden quickly placed his hands around the bird's wings. Water and mud splashed in every direction as he raised the ibis from the surface, with his net still surrounding it. As the bird's long legs seemed to strike out in every direction, the officer was grateful when the rancher ran into the water and grabbed them and its bill. Standing in almost knee-high water, the men laughed at each other before wading toward dry land.

"What do you think that bird was eating?" asked the rancher. Since the pond offered no fish, the warden guessed it had existed on insects and larvae. As it probed the mud with its bill, the ibis probably would have found enough earthworms to stay alive.

When we met the game warden later that day, we knew we had a first as far as birds were concerned. In addition to its handsome coloration, the bird had a narrow border of white feathers that went from under its chin, up around its red eyes, to the top of its bill. Only a white-faced ibis had that marking.

Feeling a calcified lump as our fingers traced the bones in each wing, we knew the bird had been grounded by a tragic break. Since it could wade far enough into the water to protect itself from coyotes and other varmints, the ibis had not yet exhausted its food source. With late spring and summer approaching, and the water dwindling, the bird was headed toward a desperate situation.

At the South Plains center in Lubbock, we learned both bad and good news. Although the wing could not be repaired, the ibis would be placed on a conservation lake at a nearby ranch. Protected by fencing, well-stocked with fish, and blessed with aquatic growth, the body of water would become the bird's permanent home.

With the fall migration from the Great Plains, flocks of white-faced ibises might choose this tranquil body of water as a resting place. Even though our bird would never join them in strong, swift flight, it could easily recognize their familiar shapes. With head and necks extended and legs trailing behind, the species would accept this earthbound cousin after their glide to earth.

63. Western Meadowlark

Sturnella neglecta

Having seen them near the tall grasses that crowded the dirt roads, the pumper loved to hear their song during his workday. Careful to avoid hitting them when they suddenly burst into the air as his truck approached, he appreciated their being an integral part of the landscape.

With an abundance of grasshoppers and beetles, leftovers from harvested grains, and seeds from miles of weeds, the birds had a smorgasbord awaiting them. Why they persisted in being so close to the road was a mystery to him.

After stopping at the tank battery, he continued his daily routine. In the distance, their distinct, individual call sounded first like a whistle and ended in a gurgle. His favorite birds were lending their musical voices to his morning.

Nearing one of the vessels, he heard the pickup coming before he saw the dust it left behind. He knew it was the same guy that raced through the farm and ranch land as if he were the only person in a hurry. As the menacing truck barreled past, dry brittle grasses and dust as well as two birds scurried in the aftermath.

"Darned idiot," he thought as he brushed the settling dust from his face and clothes. After checking the separator, he started walking back to his truck. Approaching the last tank, he scanned the ground as a matter of habit. He never took for granted that it would be snake-free.

Ahead, at the base of the metal structure, lay two birds. When closer, he realized they had to be the birds that had fled the speeding pickup. Carefully placing them in a rag that he carried for wiping his hands, he carried them to his truck.

"Two meadowlarks flew into a tank. They're still breathing," said the pumper when I answered the call. "See you in about 45 minutes."

After handing us the birds, he was visibly upset when we told him only the male survived. Paler in comparison, the female had never regained consciousness. "What about him?" Our answer was to wait and see. In a quiet, secluded area the western meadowlark would have a chance to come back slowly on his own. Food and water would be provided, but nature would determine the outcome.

Then he asked, "Why do those birds always seem to be right beside the road?" Telling him the meadowlarks try to flush insects from the grasses, we added, "They take every opportunity to eat the flesh of other birds killed on roads and highways."

While that didn't offer any comfort, it helped him realize the birds were carnivorous. However, the larks, in turn, were prey for hawks, eagles, falcons, raccoons, coyotes, and even skunks.

Before he left, the pumper took a final look at the handsomely colored lark. With its bright yellow neck, breast, and belly accented with a broad black V, the bird was attired for the breeding season. Its upper parts were a nondescript brown with buff and black markings, while the head was accented with a black-and-white-striped crown and pointed bill. Several hours later when we checked on the meadowlark, it was standing and seemed surprised by its enclosure. Examining every inch of its cage, it was impatient with its captivity.

Having placed crickets, seeds, grains, and raw beef to tempt its appetite, we were quickly informed that it did not accept our offer of help. The bird was a bundle of opposition.

Deciding to hold it until the next morning when we could take it far out in the country, we continued to observe the meadowlark from a distance. By

erate no one. Only a few other birds had been as wild and determined to mend without our assistance.

After driving to an area that offered the open grasslands the bird required, we enjoyed leaving the vehicle and hearing the silence of a country day. Not wanting to handle and frustrate the bird anymore than necessary, we gradually opened the container. All it could see was familiar terrain.

Quickly walking away with its back toward us, it stopped. Beak upward, it listened. Glancing at dried stalks and emerging greenery, the lark appeared to relax.

In the distance, there was a sound I had hoped to hear. With quick flaps of its wings, the bird rose to land on a fence post. Knowing it was back where it belonged, the meadowlark continued making its way down the fence line.

Having mastered its reintroduction to nature, the bird took flight with intermittent flapping and sailing on set wings. Prairies and plains would greet the meadowlark with abundant food and another season of courtship. The flute-like melody that announced his area was occupied would entice a future mate to share his return.

evening, the defiant guest had mastered the perches, and occasionally nibbled from the food dish. The fact that it could not see us bolstered its confidence and recovery.

Insulted with my catching it the next morning, the bird protested by kicking and nipping at any exposed flesh. Closing its cardboard carrier for the trip, I had learned quickly that these birds tol-

64. Lesser Goldfinches

Carduelis psaltria

Pounding the roof with infrequent bursts of rain, the storm lived up to the reputation given it by a weather forecaster. As it whipped the trees with what seemed like relentless winds, the violent outburst finally lessened to a typical spring shower.

Expecting the phone to ring the next morning, we were relieved by its silence. With the promise of another assault from nature following the previous night's moisture, we dreaded the predicted dust and high winds. The damp earth, dried by the force of westerly gusts, would soon be airborne. Trees once again had to withstand weather's blasts.

Following the two varying storms came a day of relative calm. We were hoping families might have been spared. The neighbor's driveway, except for a few pine needles and cones, showed no evidence that any homes had been wrecked.

The previous spring had been similar in weather events, but seemingly more destructive. When our doorbell rang a year ago, we were greeted by cupped hands protecting a small, intricately woven cup-like creation. Inside were two nestlings. Cuddled in soft rags, the tiny beings were transferred to an incubator to simulate their mother's warmth. Feeding them would be a challenge.

Since these lesser goldfinches would have been raised on unripe dandelion seeds, and regurgitated, partly digested weed and thistle seeds, we used a special dog food diet that consisted of cereal grains, vitamins, minerals, protein, and calcium. Both accepted it readily.

While the nestlings slept, we examined their miniature home. The mother bird had instinctively gathered tiny bits of twigs, dried grasses and weeds. Intertwining and compacting these materials, she had constructed a sturdy home that had to be secure during high winds.

Having gathered plant down, bits of cotton, a few small feathers, and leaves, she had created a soft cradle for her bluish-white eggs. While the opening was three inches in diameter, the depth of about an inch and a half insured that eggs and babies were protected from rolling out of the nest.

Intricate was the placement of materials. It was hard to tell where each thin blade of grass or stem began or ended. After hatching, the young would grow quickly and leave a nest that would probably never be used again.

After several feedings, our charges gained strength and actively pushed against their temporary home. Upon their arrival, we were relieved to see that their eyes were open. At least their mother was able to complete the necessary nurturing of newborns.

As more color emerged on one nestling than the other, we knew we had both female and male goldfinches. While she would develop a drab, greenish color above and dull yellow below, he would have a black cap and back. Noticeable would be his bright yellow underparts. Black wings and tail, accented with white patches, would complete his adult plumage. Even though the female's role would include future nest-building, incubation, and raising young, the male would be responsible for feeding his chosen mate someday while she raised his family. Each could contribute to future generations.

Knowing the wiggling twosome needed additional expertise as they grew, fledged, and learned how to sustain themselves, we delivered the goldfinches to the wildlife center in Lubbock. Not hearing about them for weeks was not surprising. In the mid-

dle of "baby season," the volunteers were kept busy by the daily feeding of birds and cleaning of cages.

Finally, a phone call related the outcome of our twosome. The female had failed to thrive. This phenomenon often occurred among the young. Appearing healthy one day, she had gone into a sudden decline, as if nature had sensed a weakness.

Flourishing, the male would remain until the middle of June. Strong of wing and capable of finding food, he weaned himself from the backyard feeder to join a flock of his kind. In the future, his undulating flight and high-pitched whisper would be welcome in anyone's backyard.

65. SCISSOR-TAILED FLYCATCHER

Tyrannus forficatus

As she had done the previous year, the sleek bird started building a bulky-looking cup high in the old mesquite tree. Having watched the nest grow from a few twigs, roots, and weed stems to a future home, the home-owners could enjoy another brood's success from the kitchen window.

Living in open country that offered both ranch and cropland, the woman and her husband enjoyed watching the process. When the mother bird started bringing in bits of paper, twine, rags, dry grass and cotton waste, they knew the eggs would be laid soon.

During the incubation period, the female stayed on the nest while the male not only brought her insects, but also cavorted in the sky. Having flown to a height of about 100 feet, he would plunge downward, and then turn sharply upward. As he repeated his up-and-down routine, the human family could imagine a series of Vs written in the air. Emitting a sound from his beak like a high-pitched cackle, the male ended his zigzagging on his last upward swing. Toppling backwards, he would somersault as he tumbled toward the earth. Only a jubilant father-to-be could be so happy.

Over a week had passed when an afternoon storm threatened not only the nest but the homestead as well. As the dark clouds approached from the northwest, a neighbor called the couple to warn them of a possible tornado. Seeking shelter in their storm cellar, the man and his wife took one last look at the bird in her nest.

Following nature's outrage, the door to their underground quarters opened slowly. Assured that the worst was over, the man and woman emerged. Realizing their home and beloved tree were still standing, they noticed the nest was missing.

Eager to get out of the cellar, their dog had run past them to bark at something in the tall dry grass near a fence line. Since their pet was continuously bringing them critters from the countryside, they decided to investigate. As they came to the spot where the dog was sniffing, they realized he had found the nest with the mother bird still clinging to the sides.

Realizing the bird did not seem frightened by their approach, they felt something was wrong. Carefully, the woman cupped her hands, gently raised both nest and bird, and carried them into the house.

When the call from the wildlife sanctuary in Midland notified us that the couple was bringing the bird and nest to us, we prepared an area for the expectant mother. The female scissor-tailed flycatcher appeared dazed and unresponsive. Even with insects placed close by, the bird was motionless.

A day passed with no food eaten. Fearing the worst might have happened during the night, I was greeted the next morning by the bird standing beside the nest. Expecting to see four to six creamy white eggs spotted with brown, I was shocked to find one deformed egg. Since the mother bird had abandoned it, she must have sensed that her efforts would be useless.

Not knowing if the flycatcher had recovered sufficiently for release, we called the wildlife center. They recommended we bring not only the mother bird, but also the nest and egg.

Before putting her in a carrier for the trip, we enjoyed being able once again to see the body colors in contrast to the tail of a scissor-tail. The soft gray feathers on its back and head blended into the white of its throat and breast. Its black wings were accented by its salmon-pink sides and wing linings.

Although its tail was somewhat shorter than the male's, it was typically black, long, and slender, with white outer feathers with black tips. Since flycatchers can open and shut their forked tails like a pair of scissors in flight, it was a defining part of the species.

Notable was the bird's large head and flattened bill. Bristles, or whiskers, were at the base of the beak. Although mostly seen perched on telephone wires or fences, the bird was adept at darting from a roost and catching flying insects out of the air.

After arriving at the wildlife sanctuary, a veterinarian took a blood sample to send with the egg to a lab to determine the cause of the deformity. Although we had our suspicions, the answer was long in coming.

Confirming that trace pesticides were evident, the sanctuary placed the scissor-tail in an outdoor area that permitted flight. After another evaluation of the bird, it could be released.

The species, whose presence each year announced the beginning of spring and whose absence heralded the onset of fall, faced a problem with modern technology. The graceful lady had a questionable future.

66. Pyrrhuloxia

Cardinalis sinuatus

Greeting the dawn, he looked around the yard. No one else had risen while he stood guard. Having walked, then stopped to listen and glance about, he felt confident about his domain. Beyond the fence, nothing stirred.

Soon, in a mesquite tree some distance away, another early riser stretched and shook himself awake. Hunger made him consider returning to yesterday's discovery.

With the sun getting higher in the sky, the residents, emerging from their nightly slumber, entered the yard to eat and bask in the warmth of a late spring morning. Mingling among his family members, he continued to stay alert for any danger.

When the door slammed, they looked up only long enough to see the lady headed their way. Comfortable with her presence, they knew once again she would provide their daily fare. After she opened the screen door to disappear back into the structure, they continued to enjoy a typical morning.

Approaching the fence, the stranger landed on a large wooden post. The only access to the food he sought was to go over the tightly woven mesh that stretched around the yard.

Inherent in his personality was a shy, suspicious behavior. When building a home nestled in mesquite thickets or white acacia, he and his mate knew that secrecy was a part of raising their young. Seeking food, however, had brought him to this open area.

Jumping down to the barren yard, he noticed the absence of any tall grasses. The worn earth had nothing but grains and cracked corn strewn by the woman he had seen earlier.

Insulted by this invasion and possible threat to his harem, the rooster hurried to confront the presumptuous intruder as he fed on the ground. With wings outspread and eager to fight, the barnyard fowl half-ran, half-flew, until positioned behind the uninvited guest.

Slapping the gray bird with his wing, he caused the startled diner to stumble. Stomped and pecked by the rooster, the stranger was tiring from such a beating. The much larger bird was having a devastating effect until the screen door slammed.

Screaming at the rooster to stop, the lady grabbed a broom-rake as she ran toward the fracas. As the rooster triumphantly retreated to another part of the yard, the woman feared the worst as she approached the bird. Covered

with dust, eyes closed, it appeared to be in shock.

Wrapping what looked to her like a gray cardinal in her apron, she entered the house. "I don't know if it's hurt bad or not," was the beginning of a story she related to us when she called for help.

Deep inside a cardboard box lay a male pyrrhuloxia. Similar to a northern cardinal, this bird shared the same size, but varied in beak and coloration. Accenting the back of his yellow, parrot-like bill was red that extended around his dark eyes. His crest was tipped with red. Nature had dipped a tiny brush in crimson, and lightly and unevenly painted a narrow streak downward on the feathers of the bird's breast and belly. The pyrrhuloxia was living proof of such an embellishment. The rest of the bird was gray except for tinges of red on the tail and wings.

Since we could not detect any breaks in the wings, we felt the reason the bird did not fly after being attacked was because it probably was badly bruised. Until it could feast on cotton worms, boll weevils, grasshoppers, caterpillars and weed seeds during the summer, it had been content during nesting season to chance the opportunity for grains

and seeds close to human dwellings. As fall approached, beans from mesquite and the fruit from hackberry and cactus would be added to its diet.

Keeping the bird for weeks, the wildlife sanctuary in Midland finally gave approval for its release. Having exercised in a flight cage, the pyrrhuloxia was returned to ranch land that offered thorny brush and mesquites.

Opening its carrier, we watched as the bird elevated, then continued an undulating flight. Even though it only flew for short intervals, we marveled at the considerable distance it covered.

67. Bewick's Wrens

Thryomanes bewickii

SLOWLY INCHING UP THE RAMPS AND onto the trailer, the sputtering tractor was chained in place before being turned off. Climbing down from the ornery equipment, the man was considering a tune-up for the relic when he unloaded it at his other farm.

As he walked to his pickup for the long trip west, his wife laughed and added, "When are you going to sell that old thing?" Once inside the cab, he gave her his look that implied, "When I'm ready!"

On the way home, the couple enjoyed reminiscing about their first farm. As the years

had passed, their accumulation of acreage had given them an adequate income. When drought hit one part of the state, they usually could count on their other farms to have a marketable crop.

After turning onto the dirt road that led to their home, the man welcomed the change of scenery. Thickets of prickly pear and mesquite, his barns and pastures gave him a change of pace from the hectic interstate.

While he unfastened the chains on the tractor, his wife headed into the house to prepare the evening meal. After securing the ramps, he glanced at the dry grass and twigs underneath the tattered tractor seat. "Now what kind of critter would put that up there?" he wondered. Pulling on the outermost parts, he realized how tightly matted together the materials were. "Come here a minute!" he shouted through the screen door to his wife.

"Look at that," he said, as they walked back to the tractor. Wondering what animal had gathered such an assortment of debris, they slowly started pulling twigs and grass from inside the steel support that held the seat. Even when her husband had been riding the tractor, he had not depressed this one area.

Suddenly, the entire mass slid toward her. She carefully cupped it in her hands. Leaves, hair, feathers, cotton, spider webs, and remnants of a snakeskin were intermeshed with thin bits of bark. Prying open the slightly flattened matter, she saw movement.

"Baby birds!" she repeated excitedly. "Oh, my gosh," she continued, "we left their mother at the farm!" Taking them inside, she hurried to her book on birds.

Throughout their meal, she continued to sort through pages until she confirmed her thoughts. Across the table, her husband was eager to hear about what they had. Satisfying his curiosity, she announced, "Bewick's wrens. All six of 'em."

When the call came a few days later, we were concerned when the woman related the difficulty she had encountered in feeding such tiny beings. The smallest two had not made it. To ease the guilt she was experiencing, I told her that supplementing their diet and getting the remaining nestlings to eat would be a challenge for us as well.

For three days, feedings were given from dawn to dark every thirty minutes or less, depending upon each bird. Knowing the young usually remain in the nest for fourteen days, we were halfway there.

Ready the next morning to take the birds to the South Plains center, we discovered the two youngest would not be making the trip. At least the largest and strongest had a chance.

On the way to Lubbock, we talked about our growing passengers and the adventurous locales of some of their homes. Our yard had offered houses that the wrens preferred new. Once used, they moved to the opening in a block tile fence. Over the years, people had shared their wren stories: mailboxes, flower pots, tin cans, cowboy boots, old hats, broken bottles, woodpecker holes; almost any hollow niche would do.

The most enjoyable aspects of our Bewick's wrens were their stature and melodic song. Only five inches long, with seven inches for a wingspan, the small, active birds were gray-brown on top, with white underparts. A white line was a distinguishing mark over each eye. Their long, rounded tails, tipped with white and accented with black bars, were usually carried high above their backs. Probing for insects, they used their long, slender bills to check under bark and inside last year's yucca pods.

When very young, the wrens at our house had learned their crisp, expressive tunes from the male Bewick's in the area. Clearly floating through early morning, the songs sounded like cheep, cheep, che-we-e-e-e, followed by chip, chip, chip, te-da-a, te-dee. Their voices, however, turned discordant when a coachwhip snake approached their tree house. A scolding dzz, dzz, had alerted us in time to frighten the reptile away.

By the middle of June came a report on the two survivors. Since it had a deficiency in calcium, the smaller of the two would be kept at the wildlife center in Lubbock. The other wren, which had perhaps the best chance at a normal life, was to be released during the summer. Whether it chose a tractor or a flowerpot to start another generation only nature would know for sure.

68. American Kestrels

Falco sparverius

As they approached from different directions, each found the deserted buildings to their liking. From the north, the row of hangars and the passenger lounge were beginning to show signs of neglect. Although they had been an active part of the community's life, they no longer seemed needed after the airport closed. "Just the location we've been looking for," thought the man.

From the south, the empty buildings were surrounded by open fields with rose-colored thistles blooming among yellow wildflowers and spring grasses. With no human activity, insects, rodents, and birds had reclaimed the undisturbed growth. Having looked at all the possibilities, she decided on the building with the easiest access.

With time, each thought the decision to relocate had been a wise one. Except for the wind and an occasional dust storm, both felt as if they had the place to themselves. Although isolated, the hangar offered the space he needed. She liked the security, since no one would notice her comings and goings.

Over a month had passed when one morning she heard a noise on the great expanse that had no grass. A long, slender object would go back and forth over the flat, dark gray surface. After a while, it went back inside the hangar and the rest of the day was quiet. As long as the thing went back in its hole, she felt safe.

As soon as the man and his crew completed one job, another challenge would arrive. The steady flow of business made their days pass quickly. Only when a delivery was due did they have a chance to stop and talk. Loving what they did was compensation enough.

After telephoning for advice and possible assistance, a male voice mentioned Team Development and the location. "We try to keep a low profile, so I'd appreciate your help," he added. Telling him it would take us about twenty minutes, I motioned for Art to get our equipment.

On the drive to the old county airport, he was eager to learn about the unusual phone call. "The man said Indy cars! As in racing," I answered. Dumbfounded, we could hardly believe Indianapolis race cars were in the county. Pausing for a moment, I added, "He has what he thinks is a baby hawk."

Walking into the hangar, we entered another world. In front of us were two Indy cars. Long, low and streamlined, they looked as if they would barely fit us. While two crewmen continued to work, the man gave us a gracious welcome. Leading us over to a workbench filled with tools, he reached for a cardboard box lined with paper towels. Inside was a feathering kestrel.

Pointing toward faded yellow insulation that hung from an opening at the top of the wall, the man explained that the bird had been able to flutter enough to break its fall. Outside, we could see that the roof and the walls did not meet perfectly. This would have enabled birds to use the space and its insulating qualities for their new families.

"Here's another one," called one of the crew from the hangar. "Just seemed to float right down from up there," he continued. Obviously, the nestlings were anxious to test their wings. The two daredevils might have siblings, so one of the men climbed a ladder to the opening. Carefully inserting his hand, he could feel two more nestlings hiding inside.

Realizing this was no place for baby birds or ill-tempered parents, the man asked if we would take the young and

insure their safety. Since he had not seen either of the parents, we felt the nestlings' food had been brought to the opening outside. Curiosity had led to the exploration in the other direction and their surprise visit.

With the foursome cradled in a carrier, we thanked the man for helping to assure the kestrels' well-being. Explaining that these small falcons had been fed insects the first week of their lives, we said they were now being given insects and mice several times a day. Even when they left the nest, their parents would continue feeding them for a week or so until they learned to hunt.

As we started to leave, the man shared with us that he and his crew tune high- performance engines that could only be released from their shop after testing on the runways. The isolated location was necessary for scheduling and to keep the curious away.

Admiring his expertise and knowledge of such complicated machines, we promised to keep his unusual secret. Memorial Day races in the future, however, took on a different meaning as we recalled specialized fliers, both on a race track and in the skies.

69. BLUE JAY

Cyanocitta cristata

Throughout the morning, the two youngsters explored the fenced enclosure. No longer depending upon their first home, they enjoyed new discoveries while their mother was away. When she returned with a treat for each, she gently scolded them for being out in the middle of the lawn. Hungry for the food she carried, they were easily coaxed toward a shaded area offered by a large yaupon.

With each trip, their mother had encouraged a short flight from the shrub to the live oak tree nearby. Finally, the attempt was made. Each in turn managed to reach a lower limb.

The seemingly carefree twosome continued to frolic among the branches whenever their mother left for a while. Once back, she would fly directly to the oak after hearing their welcoming cries.

As we watched from the den window, we felt some anxiety whenever the mother bird left the yard. Our neighborhood was fairly safe, but there was always the possibility of an unwelcomed visitor.

"Keep an eye on those two," I begged Art, as I walked toward an insistent phone. With his camera in hand, he would not have wanted to leave their first attempt at independence.

Begging me to take a fledgling, the caller was nearly hysterical. Neighborhood felines frequented her flower beds, trees, and even her roof in their relentless search for the young and vulnerable. The bird would not stand a chance, she added.

The familiar seasonal request for us to take fledglings that were learning how to fly was difficult to call. Letting parents teach their young was essential in nature.

Even in our own situation, we faced the ultimate reality that not all young birds would succeed. Trying to analyze each individual problem sometimes resulted in our relenting from the most difficult of decisions.

To accept a fledgling meant denying a parent the privilege of raising its own. Often we were tempted to intervene. Ultimately, we realized we had to wait for the scenario to play itself out.

An hour later, the doorbell rang. After telling us that she had spent a good amount of time chasing the young bird, the caller had trapped the fledgling.

Inside a shoe box was a blue jay still damp from the perspiration of the woman's hand. Upon further examination, I noticed that one wing did not

extend as far as the other. Whether this had been caused by its capture or not I would never know.

Saddened by the fact that another creature had been taken from nature, I realized pet owners were lax in controlling their cats. To have an indoor feline would be too much of an inconvenience. Instead, the animal was free to roam, maim, and kill. Subject to various diseases from the feral cats of any neighborhood, the pet would also be in violation of many cities' animal ordinances.

Once the woman had left, I prepared an area for the blue jay. Since no obvious breaks had been detected, we felt the wing might have been bruised. As I reached inside the box, a nip on the hand and a raucous protest ensued. With feet flailing, the angry, vocal jay was adamant in its denial of wanting to be with us.

Even its juvenile plumage indicated what was to come. The crested head, back, wings and tail would become a bright blue. It already sported the black necklace that crossed its breast before heading upward toward the back of the head. Its gray-white underparts would be drab in comparison to the accents of black and white barring on its wings and tail.

The jay's natural diet was varied. Loving acorns, corn, and seeds, the bird also accepted insects, spiders, small mice, and unfortunately small birds and eggs. Where available, wild grapes enhanced its menu. As long as backyard feeders offered suet, sunflower seeds, and peanuts, the blue jay would consider a stopover.

Offering crickets, grasshoppers, baby mice, corn, and seeds, I noticed the noisy jay would accept the food when I wasn't looking. However, if it caught my eye, the bird would quickly snub my efforts and me.

From the kitchen, I could hear it mimic the outside birds that it heard. If children on their bicycles were too loud as they coursed down our street, the jay in its own aggressive way shrieked at these intruders.

Changing its water and food dishes became a daily battle. Harsh screams were common, and the longer it stayed, I questioned anyone ever wanting one as a pet. Perhaps it was only practicing the ear-piercing cries to prepare itself for release. While the delivery of this raucous house guest to South Plains brought relief to our ears, we missed its daily shenanigans in trying to dominate any other birds in our care.

After holding it for over a month, the director of the wildlife center in Lubbock decided the injury to the jay's wing was permanent. Although it could elevate to lower perches in an aviary, the bird was not accomplished in the flight necessary for living in the wild. It would never have the ability to dive-bomb and peck squirrels, cats, even humans in defense of its young.

A decision was made to keep the colorful character. As a buddy for another jay that could not be released, it not only would provide company, but the two permanent residents would be mentors to nestlings in the future. Teaching future blue jays, our protégé could make sure that jays released to the wild might be destined to be a cat's worst enemy.

70. Western Screech Owl & American Kestrel

Megascops kennicottii & Falco sparverius

As the winds increased, the bird huddled against the trunk of a live oak. Unable to find a woodpecker's hole, it gripped a branch with its large feet as tightly as it could.

Increasing in velocity, the gusts shook the canopy that provided not only a daytime refuge, but also protection from the rain and small hail that followed. After swaying and undulating violently, the tree returned to its statuesque presence beside the river.

Fluffing its feathers into their proper place again, the bird sidled away from the center of the oak. Since its hunting for rodents and insects had been postponed because of the storm, it jumped into a void in the tree and made a rapid descent to the ground.

When the homeowner looked through her picture window toward the river, she noticed a small gray bird standing on the lawn. Quietly opening the backdoor, the woman realized the visitor to her backyard was an owl. Since its eyes were closed, she wondered if it had been a victim of the turbulent winds.

Having promised severe weather, the forecasters had been accurate as to its intensity. Thus, Diane Tracy's call from San Angelo was not unexpected. Working within the guidelines of my state permit, she had received from Parks & Wildlife a fledgling kestrel and a screech owl. When we met her and husband, Dale, in Sterling City, she added that she had been told the owl was found on someone's lawn near the river.

Inside a carrier, the small raptor, which we assumed was a western screech owl, stared at us with its bright yellow eyes. With mottled gray wing feathers and heavily streaked chest and belly, it resembled an upright chunk of tree bark. Accents included white spots on its shoulders, a dark facial rim, black bill, and ear tufts that could be upright or almost hidden.

After our menu of small mice had been devoured, we took the screech owl and the kestrel to Gail Barnes at the Lubbock center. Placing the kestrel with other fledglings, she wondered if the owl might possibly be a whiskered screech owl. Wanting to contact an ornithologist with Texas Tech University in Lubbock for a positive identification, she promised to call.

Placed in a mew after a thorough examination, the owl surprised Gail by its flight ability. She phoned to say she could find nothing wrong with it. The ornithologist verified the bird as a first-year, female, western screech owl that had strayed. Placement in a heavily-forested area in the Davis Mountains, or further west, would be appropriate.

A question continued to plague me: Where on the Concho River was the screech owl found? Through Diane's persistence, we discovered the owl had not been found in San Angelo, but Christoval, some fourteen miles to the south.

With this information, Gail contacted the ornithologist again. Could the western screech owl be released where it was found? She immediately told us the good news.

During its two-week stay in Lubbock, the owl exercised and "fattened up" on a nightly menu of baby mice. Ready for its return to the tree-lined river in Christoval, we checked weather reports before heading south.

On a week day, the heavily timbered riverside park was deserted except for one campsite. Towering live oaks and pecans lent shade to an undergrowth of buckeyes. After research on everyone's part, it was definitely a suitable area for the smallest of owls.

Although it was a very breezy day, the huge trees offered a fairly calm environment under their spreading limbs and foliage. Opening the carrier gate, I could see the owl glaring intently at me through the sides of the container. It didn't budge.

Deciding to take the top off, we loosened the side closures. The owl continued to stare at me with total disdain.

When Gail mentioned it had given her "the eye," I was uncertain until that moment just what she meant. The owl's total aloofness and contempt was directed toward me. Then it glanced upward and saw the trees.

Having a choice of a straight or crooked trail to freedom, the bird chose the latter. Banking first to the left, then right, its silent wings propelled it around and through the understory growth as it rose quickly to disappear among the trees. In seconds, its lengthy odyssey had ended.

71. Curve-billed Thrashers

Toxostoma curvirostre

After dark, the caller said she had two rather large baby birds. Their nest had been located about seven to eight feet above the ground. In their nearly naked condition, the nestlings had evidence of feathers just breaking the skin. The woman had seen no other young or the parents.

A short time later, she arrived with the twosome carefully wrapped in a soft cloth. The older bird opened its eyes, and then closed them as if in a deep sleep. With no response from the younger sibling, I cautioned their mentor as to its survivability during the night. Having probably been fed more and stronger, the larger baby had a chance.

Discovering the younger bird had not made it through the night, I began a routine for the remaining one. Force-feeding it the soft parts of mashed insects every forty-five minutes, I noticed that although it swallowed, it was barely responding to any nutrition.

Calling that night, the woman said she had found another one. Glad to learn that at least one had survived so far, she delivered the third member of such an unfortunate family.

The next morning little response came from either of the nestlings. Although they had been fed, and snuggled close together, they did not react to my touch or movement of their nest. Having to drive to another city to pick up a hawk, I decided to let nature take care of what I expected to happen.

That afternoon, with the bird of prey settled into his new accommodations, I knew I had to deal with the inevitable. As I moved the nest I had made in an old basket, the nestlings' heads popped straight up with mouths open.

Surprised by this sudden burst of life, I felt their recovery was partially due to the long rest they had during the morning and early afternoon. Although they made no sounds, they were eager for nourishment. Once satisfied, they slept again.

Having asked initially if such large babies were grackles, the lady had seemed pleased to learn they were not. Considered songbirds, the nestlings, with their yellow mouths, were thrashers. Hatched from pale blue to bluish-green eggs with tiny spots of brown, the birds would normally remain in their nest for at least 18 days. They appeared to be about a week old.

Soon, not only had they progressed from cricket guts to the entire insect, the nestlings had found their voices. The older bird was more vocal, while the younger tried copying the sounds it heard.

Out of the nest and onto the perches, the twosome was well-feathered after their two-week stay. Knowing a lack of parents and avian nurturing seemed to slow their progress, the new fledglings needed the company of others and the space for strengthening flight.

Having thought the young birds might be sage thrashers, I learned at South Plains Wildlife Center that they were our more familiar curve-billed thrashers. Gray-brown and lighter underneath, the birds had the typical spotting on breast and sides that denotes a member of the thrush family.

When mature, they would be larger than a mockingbird. Their long tails, dark curved bills, and yellow eyes would add to their distinguishing characteristics. Unlike the mocker, they would not have as notable a set of wing bars.

Once free, these thrashers would devour insects, larvae, fruits, and berries. As they searched the ground for grubs and ants, holes would be dug by their strong beaks quickly tossing dirt and leaves aside. Striking sideways the debris left from another season, the birds would be relentless in finding nature's hidden treasures.

72. Barn Owl

Tyto alba

In the southwest, the clouds continued to build during the afternoon. Maybe this summer storm would not rain itself out before reaching the hills and bluffs near town. We hoped for a drenching shower. Just before the wind laid, a cool breeze preceded what was to come.

Following the calm, dusty gusts slammed against windows and caused doors to whine. Often described as a "blow with no show," the winds played havoc with our trees. Finally, raindrops, sounding like hail, pounded the house.

After the storm had hurried on to the northeast, it left behind moist, fresh air and a vivid sunset. Tomorrow would be soon enough to gather the small, broken limbs and leaves that littered our yard.

"Didn't find it 'til after the rain," said the woman, who called about a bird. The previous evening, after the storm, she had gone out to check on her horses and a family of barn owls.

"Are the owls in your stable?" I asked. "No, they were born and raised on the bluff behind the barn. I've watched those young birds since they hatched. Even now, fully feathered, they stay in those holes during the day."

Continuing her story, she told of walking through the stalls to the backside of the structure. She wanted to make sure her owls were still in the natural crèches. As she counted the family members, she realized one was missing from the ledge. Only then did she look at the large growth of prickly pear.

Stuck between two large pads was one of the juveniles born that spring. The woman felt it had been blown into the cactus by the storm. Long, sharp spines kept the owl from escaping. Knowing the bird probably had been impaled by some of the thorns, she started tearing off pads in order to free the miserable youngster.

Once she had reached the bird, she broke away the growth that held the owl captive. Placing the bird against her hip, she held it with one hand while trying to exit without too many more barbs in her hands and legs.

Leaving the dense cactus, she started pulling thorns out of the owl. "When I finished him, I started on me," she added. Uncertain if smaller spines were in the bird and what effects they might have, she decided to call.

As she led us through the stable, the stalls, with their numerous timbers for roosting, offered a perfect home for barn owls. Even in daytime, the structure was dark and aromatic from hay, dust, and horses.

After walking through the north opening, we were once again in bright sunshine. Looking toward the northeast, we saw the large prickly pear growing at the base of the bluff that towered some twenty-five feet above.

The earthen home for the owls was a secure place for this family. Whether it had been formed by man or nature, the steep face kept predators from reaching the nestlings and fledglings. Time, storms, erosion, and usage had created a novel approach to family planning.

The bluff's mixture of clay, rocks, sandstone, and old roots was a faded terra cotta in color. The recesses could have been formed by gully washers as rainwater plummeted to the floor below. Undermined plants and dislodged small boulders might have been discarded as the face of the bluff evolved.

To imagine the ordeal suffered by the woman and the owl while they battled the cactus made us appreciate the tenacity of both. We promised to call back with details from the wildlife center.

Searching for any remaining thorns in the owl, we realized the woman had removed the majority of the painful spines. With the overlooked ones extracted, the bird rested and was fed three days before being taken to the South Plains Rehab Center in Lubbock.

The following week, the manager of the center called to say the barn owl was ready for release. When a center volunteer delivered the bird, we took her with us to see the unusual nursery.

Even though it had hatched on a narrow ledge of the bluff and was familiar with the terrain, the owl refused to fly. Knowing it had accessed its natal home previously, we were horrified when it hopped and ran toward the prickly pear.

Using a pole net and patience, we were able to recapture the bird without a bout with the cactus. Loading the owl for its return trip to Lubbock, the volunteer and we knew that not all releases are successful.

Later, the barn owl, accompanied by four other juveniles, would be returned to the area. During a still, moonlit night, they discovered the overwhelming lure of open country and good hunting.

73. House Wrens

Troglodytes aedon

"HEARD HIM BEFORE I SAW HIM," was her description of the petite songbird as it darted around in the barn. Watching the male bring twigs and sticks he had gathered outside, she knew it was building more than one nest to tempt a mate.

Soon debris could be seen under the center of a saddle tucked away on a shelf. Unable to locate another nest, she assumed the bird was content with that area. It wasn't until a week later that she noticed activity coming

HER ALARM

CAME FROM THE

NOTICEABLE

BULGE OF

 WHATEVER IT

HAD JUST

SWALLOWED...

and going from a row of pipes stacked near the entrance.

Once the bird had left, the woman decided to check the ends of the pipes. Finally, she found the newly placed nesting materials tightly interlocked in one of the openings. Knowing courtship would soon begin, she looked forward to watching the couple's antics.

Outside, the newly arrived female lit on a fence post. Wings quivering, she greeted the male. With his tail and wings spread, he approached her with his head held back. His song left no doubt of his intentions.

Introducing his intended to the nests he had built, the male had already established his territory. Telling other birds through song that the barn was taken, he dominated his domain with persistent singing and occasional scolding when other birds came too close.

When the woman checked on the nest a week later, she marveled at its construction. Except for its narrow opening, it was well-concealed. Previously, she had noticed the female arriving with bits of dry grass, small leaves, weeds, and feathers.

With a flashlight, she saw two of several eggs inside. Cream-colored and totally speckled with tiny dots of cinnamon-brown, the eggs promised a future generation.

After two weeks, the coming and going of the parents increased, with innumerable trips to supply the appetites of the newly hatched. Watching the parents arrive with moths, butterflies, spiders, ladybugs, and small grasshoppers, the woman knew the nestlings were well-fed.

Her appreciation of the parents grew even more as she happened to notice that the young were fed more in the morning than during the heat of the afternoon. During the lull, the parents rested.

Suddenly, the woman's life and that of the birds changed. A phone call and a predator prompted a late evening conversation I could never have anticipated.

Not expecting to be informed that a relative in Phoenix was near death, the woman was making hurried plans for the long drive when she decided to check on the family in the barn. Wanting to wish them well, she was horrified to see a large snake slithering away from the pipe and into a stack of hay. Her alarm came from the noticeable bulge of whatever it had just swallowed.

With only one parent remaining, the woman felt it would be impossible for the young birds to receive enough food. She wanted to bring us the nestlings the next day. After being asked where she lived, the frustrated lady answered, "Paradise."

My mind went blank. "Where is that?" I asked. "We're south of

Decatur. We need to head to Weatherford, straight down Interstate-20 to you, and on to Phoenix." Informing her that she could take the nestlings to a rehabilitation center in Dallas, she said that would be going in the opposite direction. Besides, there was all that traffic. She had to reach Arizona in a hurry.

When I agreed to meet her at the truck stop the next day, the distraught woman was relieved. "Call you when I'm a few miles away," were her parting words.

Fortunate to be in the care of someone who fed them during their westward journey, four house wrens greeted me with open mouths and insatiable hunger. From a sparse natal down, brownish in color, the nestlings were beginning to feather. Soon they would be brownish above, a paler grayish-brown below. Their rufous flanks would be especially noticeable when their blackish barred wings and tail were spread.

After the woman continued on her journey, we welcomed the travelers with small crickets. Their parents had completed a critical phase of their development, and the kind mentor had insured their survival.

At the wildlife center in Lubbock, the director and volunteers continued to meet the demands of the growing foursome. Upon release, the little wrens someday might breed as far north as southern Canada and winter as far south as Mexico. With nature's insects and freedom, they had found another paradise.

UPON RELEASE, THE LITTLE WRENS SOMEDAY MIGHT BREED AS FAR NORTH AS SOUTHERN CANADA AND WINTER AS FAR SOUTH AS MEXICO...

74. Great horned Owl

Bubo virginianus

After fluffing his feathers and wiggling his tail, the large bird leapt from atop a mesquite tree to begin his nightly hunt. Effortlessly, his powerful wings soon attained the height he needed. Gliding between the rising giants, he sailed over the escarpment. Descending toward a building in the distance, he sought the food source attracted by its outdoor lighting.

Hatched on a rocky ledge over which he had just flown, he had grown from a downy chick in January to a sizeable bird of prey by June. Having wings and a tail developed enough for flight, he began the adventures of locating and recognizing his nightly quest for food. With his parents' guidance, he had mastered the most essential element of his behavior.

When rabbits were scarce, the juvenile had learned, through the summer months and into September, small rodents and beetles were available near the dumpster behind the building.

Gliding toward that area, he was startled by the opening of a door. Silently veering away from the man disposing of trash, the bird chose a different approach to the area he sought.

With his exceptional vision, he soon noticed the movement of a creature scurrying toward the receptacle. Intent upon clasping the animal in his talons, he slammed into a barrier he had not seen.

As the rat hurried away from his near-death, the bird tried to regain his composure. In spite of his throbbing left wing, he was determined to take flight. Starting forward and flapping his wings, he could not lift his heavy body from the ground. Having fallen after the impact, he shook his dusty feathers. He could only stand and wait for what might happen next.

"Wind plant," said the manager when he called. "Looks like a great horned owl. It hit the chain-link fence," he continued. With his directions, we drove east, then south, to the turnoff. Waiting at the locked gate for

the man to arrive, we enjoyed the arid beauty of this desert scrubland.

Following the manager's pickup, we traveled on a recently built caliche road. As we skirted the southern end of the Flanigan, a catch basin for the water district, we could see the building and the windmills in the distance.

Huddled against the steel links of the fence, the owl hissed and popped his bill as we approached. Trying to keep his distance from us, he followed the fence line with a hurried walk. We hoped the extent of his injury was bruising rather than a fracture as he held his wings equally to his body. With Art's and the manager's assistance in corralling the bird, I was able to place a net over the owl as he continued to protest.

Feeling no breaks, we could tell the juvenile had adequate body fat by feeling the areas adjacent to his breastbone or keel. His development of winter plumage was nearly complete. Resembling an adult great horned owl, he had a white throat patch, barred wings and tail.

After we delivered the owl to the wildlife center in Lubbock, news came that the great horned owl had suffered a soft-tissue injury. With time, he would recover.

Weeks later, we brought the bird back for release. Since we arrived home late in the evening, we placed the great horned in a larger and more comfortable cage than his carrier. The owl dined on mice during the night. The next evening the manager had arranged for us to release the bird on the wind farm lease.

Ready to load the juvenile, I was greeted by the most hostile and aggressive great horned owl I was ever to handle. As I opened the door, the bird lunged at my head and shoulders with talons extended. Not in the mood for another trip, the bird of prey attacked several times. Only a thick towel thrown over his head and leather gloves for protection helped me capture his legs and bring him out of the enclosure. The strength of his protesting legs was matched by the strong flapping of his wings. He was ready.

When we arrived at the release site, a number of employees and their families greeted us. To see a great horned owl from a close perspective had been promised. With this bird I could not chance a mishap. One wrong move on my part could enable the bird a chance to fly and inflict cuts on someone else.

Choosing safety over a display of such an unruly bird of prey, we had our audience stand aside while we opened the carrier. Bursting away from us and toward open country, the owl flew over the greasewood and cactus. Landing among the native plants several hundred feet away, the bird was hidden from view.

"What's it doing now?" asked a young boy. Telling the families the bird was "getting its bearings," Art stressed that it would take some time for it to become familiar with its surroundings. "Won't a coyote or fox get it?" Informing them that very few animals would approach such a formidable opponent, we felt confident in its abilities to protect itself.

When a rather tall man said he couldn't see it anymore, we stressed that was the importance of its coloration. Blending into its surroundings was part of its defense. As we left the area, neither of us could see the owl even though we knew where it had landed. Its disappearance into the wild was reassuring.

Extending an invitation to learn about the wind farm and ride the elevator to the top of a windmill, the manager later took each of us on a tour inside the tower. After lifting a floor hatch, he noted I was 275 feet above the ground. Then climbing a short way, he opened a door to the top. With head and shoulders above the sleek, white skin of the bus-sized housing for the generator, I could see to the east the picturesque hills that led to Signal Peak. At last I felt akin to the owl that had brought me to this locale.

Understanding the beauty of the terrain the owl traversed nightly in his flights over the bluffs, I realized the depth of his untamable spirit.

75. Cactus Wrens

Campylorhynchus brunneicapillus

Undisturbed by any human activity, the bird had commenced to build its nest in the cholla cactus near the well site. Idle from the bust days of the '80s, the pump jack was silent. Nearby, the tanks and separator stood vigil over a time past.

Grasses and cactus had reclaimed their native soil. The once-cleared caliche drive was nearly hidden by knee-high grasses and weeds. An occasional lonely mesquite offered the only shade for miles.

Landing on one of the many branches of the plant, the bird seemed oblivious to the projecting thorns. Dry blades of grass and plant stems were carefully placed where the cholla offered the best support. When he finished laying the bottom of his nest, the bird began shaping the sides which would be protected by the prickly branches of the plant.

Shaped, woven, and rounded into a large domed structure, the materials he used had been converted into thick, matted walls. Next, the bird created an opening a few inches above the inner chamber. By the time his effort was completed, the architect had completed a tunnel large enough to accommodate his mate and himself.

From the outside, only a large hole appeared to lead inside. However, not being able to see the future eggs and nestlings would prevent winged predators from easily taking his family. The cholla would serve as a natural defense from four-legged critters.

Having built several other nests, he had a choice to make. The unused nests would make ideal roosting sites or future nesting areas if a second or third brood occurred. With his attracted mate, a decision was made.

Once the nest had been lined with feathers, four eggs were laid. In such a remote dwelling, only nature and the parents could appreciate their creamy-white to pinkish shells spotted with a reddish-brown.

Soon, the parents were scurrying to provide small insects and worms for their growing nestlings. Even bread crumbs thrown out for the sparrows at a nearby farm house were gathered. Days passed quickly.

One morning, voices suddenly startled the mother bird. Hidden inside the tunnel, she noticed two men standing by the metal structures. Searching for food, her mate had not yet returned. As the men turned to leave, she heard a loud noise approaching her nest.

Frightened by a large, yellow, bellowing piece of equipment that came within a few feet of her home, she instinctively darted from the mouth of the tunnel and quickly flew away.

As the long, sharp blade cleared the grasses and prickly-pear cactus surrounding the well site, the operator turned and maneuvered the machine toward the large cholla near the corner of the caliche pad. Hearing the machine suddenly stop, the two men turned to see the operator climbing down and walking toward the large cactus.

"Looked like a straw football caught in that cholla," was the description the worker gave when he called about the nest. "Couldn't see anything through that hole, but could hear 'em," he continued.

Since the company had a required clearance for the numerous trucks and service vehicles, he had to remove the cholla. Wearing gloves, he slowly snapped the branches away from the nest. With the thorns piercing the leather, he had to stop and pull them out of his hands and the gloves before proceeding. Finally, he was able to free the entire nest from its spiny confinement.

Leaving the youngsters inside, he

wondered whether the parents would return to the nest with so much anticipated noise and activity. To place it far enough away from the normal routine of activating a site meant they might be abandoned in the process.

Approval from his boss, who had called Parks & Wildlife, came readily. Within two hours, he was delivering the bulky nest and its cargo to our front door. Inside, the four cactus wrens had developed into small miniatures of their parents. Although their coloration was duller and fainter, by winter their plumage would be almost like the adults. Only the black markings on a white throat were absent.

Borderline fledglings, the foursome devoured our cricket cache readily. Although they would have followed their parents back to the nest at night, they seemed to enjoy our large cage, varied perches, and constant feeding.

Notable were their rusty brown caps, backs, wings, and tails, white stripes over each eye, pale underparts, and spotted breasts. Their wings and tails were barred with black and white. Long, curved bills, rounded tails, and body size would someday have them misidentified as thrashers rather than wrens.

Needing the expertise of the wildlife center in Lubbock, the cactus wrens thrived in a spacious aviary. With eagerness, they learned to hunt for their food on the dirt floors. As in nature,

they were provided with a leaf, grass or hay-strewn environment. Poking their beaks underneath the debris, they could search for hidden insects. Their curiosity and willingness to investigate were essential for their release and survival.

76. Black Vulture

Coragyps atratus

When I heard her voice, I expected another hawk or owl. Instead, our link with San Angelo, Diane Tracy held a unique experience for us.

Not knowing what to do with a large black bird, Animal Control had called her earlier and asked, "Do you want it?" They knew it couldn't fly, but could see no obvious compound fracture on either wing. Telling them she was on her way, she grabbed her leather gloves and a carrier.

After hearing her warning that the bird would eject whatever it had in its stomach as a defensive move, the officers gladly stepped back and allowed her the privilege. Grasping the scavenger with its head pointed away from her, she removed it from its metal confinement.

Having checked her bird books, she was confident that the raptor was a black vulture. When she related this bit of news, I challenged her thinking with the fact that turkey vultures, when young, have a black head that reddens with maturity. "This bird is different," was her reply.

Since we had only seen black vultures along the Big Bend portion of the Rio Grande and knew the Panhandle and West Texas were dominated by

the turkey vulture, we were eager to see her bird of prey. Not only did we need to verify her identification, we carried two bird books because of our own lack of experience with that specie.

When we met her in Sterling City for a transfer, we realized immediately that the bird was not a turkey vulture. Temperament and the head were the first indications. With grace, the vulture slowly placed one foot in front of the other as it came toward the carrier's gate. With the tip of its bill, it carefully felt of this barrier to its freedom.

Before removing it from the container, I noticed the small, naked, gray head. In the late morning sunlight, it almost appeared to have a silvery sheen. As the skin wrinkled downward from the back of the eyes to cover the entire neck, it reminded me of the days of chivalry. Knights had worn a camail, an open-faced hood woven with metal links for protection. We were in the presence of royalty.

With both hands firmly holding the wings to its body, I moved the vulture to an open towel. Placing it upside down, we extended the wings. The white linings on its outer primaries, and the short, almost square end of its tail, confirmed the identification. Since Diane had mentioned the vulture was extremely thin, we agreed after feeling its breast bone.

To be so depleted of body fat, the raptor wasn't lacking in any strength in its wings. Having pushed so hard against my hands that I feared it would squirm loose, I could well imagine an even stronger, healthier bird lifting its four-to six-pound body to great heights.

Since the wildlife center in Lubbock had never had a black vulture, we made arrangements to meet the manager's husband, Larry, halfway in Lamesa. Upon seeing the bird, he had the same impression of the outstanding differences between a turkey vulture and a black vulture.

The drive home gave me time to recall the courtship of this specie. Similar to the days of yore, winning a female's favor required a display. While knights might impress their ladies with gallantry, the avian rendition was one of strutting with wings partly spread. Sidling toward her with head bobbing, a male could not be discouraged by her turning her back and flying away. Persistence in approaching the reluctant lady and bowing like an underling often won her favor.

Nuptials were finalized by a remarkable flight together. Circling and sailing in spirals, one followed the other as if skaters in the sky. Finally, the couple would fly away and stay together while raising the young.

Calling to discuss her findings, the manager, Gail Barnes, had discovered an old, calcified break in one of the vulture's wings. The bird had been down for some time. Its thinness was due to an inability to find enough food. Her diagnosis would be confirmed by one of the veterinarians later in the week. Since the raptor could not be released, it was the consensus of the previous and current directors, as well as Gail's, that the bird should be kept for educational purposes.

Placed in its own mew, the black vulture would be given plenty of time to gain weight. Later, if it and two turkey vultures would tolerate each other's company, the bird would share a mew and companionship.

Knowing, however, that in the wild, black vultures take advantage of turkey vultures' more developed sense of smell in finding food, and bully them away from a carcass, we felt only time would tell if two are company and three a crowd. If that occurred, the black vulture would receive its own mew.

Before we ended our phone conversation, Gail said she thought the graceful raptor was a female. The vulture's regal countenance and deportment would determine her future as Lady Black.

77. Greater Roadrunner

Geococcyx californianus

"THE RUCKUS IN MY BACKYARD would have woke the devil," started the woman in trying to describe what had happened to a bird. "By the time I reached the dog, he had it in his mouth. But my cat was the one that pulled out all those feathers."

After arriving at her home, we marveled at her animated description of her pets' misbehavior. Both animals had apparently been watching while the bird methodically ran a few feet, took several steps, and stopped. Looking about, it then walked a few more steps, before stopping, listening, and watching in hopes of

flushing out an insect or lizard.

Her ancient feline had slowly crossed the lawn in hopes of a diversion. Quietly sneaking up behind the hunting bird, the cat had pounced at the preoccupied intruder of its backyard. Age and inactivity, however, had slowed its reflexes. Instead of landing on the bird's body, the cat hit squarely on top of one of the bird's wings. Suddenly held to the ground by this threatening weight, the bird turned to pummel the feline's face with its long beak. As it twisted to strike again, it left behind underneath the cat a good portion of its wing feathers.

Having struck the cat's tender nose and then its upper lip, the roadrunner pecked an even harder blow above one eye. Backing away from the unexpected retaliation, the cat tried once again to catch the elusive bird. After landing on the roadrunner's tail, it was surprised when the long feathers remained under its two front feet as the bird escaped.

The commotion had already gained the attention of the woman's dog. Seeing the bird escape the cat, the canine intercepted the roadrunner. Proud of such a catch, the animal carried its prize to its owner coming out the back door.

Wet with saliva, the bird was dropped at the woman's feet. As she screamed at both pets, the shamed dog went to hide under the hedge.

AGE AND

INACTIVITY,

HOWEVER, HAD

SLOWED ITS

REFLEXES. INSTEAD

OF LANDING ON

THE BIRD'S BODY,

THE CAT HIT

SQUARELY ON

TOP OF ONE

OF THE BIRD'S

WINGS...

Taking the beat-up chaparral inside and placing it in a shoe box, the woman returned to the backyard to admonish her children. Seeing the dog with its tail tightly curled between its legs, she could sense its remorse. As she gathered the cat into her arms, she suddenly realized that her old-timer was no match for the determined roadrunner.

Slightly bleeding, the cuts on its nose and lip were noticeable. Beginning to swell, the area above the eye might require a visit to the vet. As soon as she handed us the roadrunner, which by this time was protesting its confinement, she left with her defeated warrior.

Once home, we carefully opened the box. The young roadrunner resembled its parents, except for total length. As it matured, it would be almost two feet long. Half of that length would be tail.

Its crested head had the white, blue, and orange patch behind each eye. Buff underneath, with black, bronze, and buff breast feathers, the bird sported the typical black and white back accented with feathers lending a blue, green, and bronze iridescence. Its shaggy, streaked appearance gave it the ability to blend into its surroundings. Missing were most of its tail feathers and all but one of the primaries on its left wing.

Someday, its long legs and trim body would lend to its speed. Its large feet and long stride would be necessary in catching grasshoppers, mice, small snakes, horned lizards, even scorpions and centipedes. Once the missing feathers were replaced, the roadrunner would exhibit coordination and balance to be envied.

Looking for any puncture wounds inflicted by the cat, we found none. The woman's quick response to her backyard free-for-all had possibly spared the roadrunner from infection. Upon placing the bird in a carrier, we noticed it walked with a limp on the same side as the missing wing feathers.

Taking the roadrunner to the Lubbock wildlife center, we knew it would be afforded the time and support needed to recuperate. Since no one could say for sure that the cat had been unsuccessful in puncturing the skin, the bird was placed on antibiotics. After a lengthy stay, the roadrunner, with its tail extended and head looking straight ahead, ventured forth into a release site that offered a terrain vital to its survival.

TAKING THE ROADRUNNER TO THE LUBBOCK WILDLIFE CENTER, WE KNEW IT WOULD BE AFFORDED THE TIME AND SUPPORT NEEDED TO RECUPERATE.

78. Forster's Tern

Sterna forsteri

The drive to Andrews was one of his favorites. Surrounded by natural and man-made terrain, he relished being away from the noise and congestion of an interstate. Watching the countryside change from mesquite, cactus, and scrub oak to grasslands and plowed fields, he always looked forward to the fenced rangeland that seemed endless.

The lull in truck traffic gave him time to wonder about the families that had occupied the old, deserted frame houses along the way. On one trip he had discovered a large, round water tank hidden among fairly tall trees, knee-high dried nettle, and seeding grasses. Its rusted sides were indicative of the moist ground that had encouraged the growth of the now-towering foliage.

The morning offered little traffic on the two-lane highway. As he neared the area he knew to be north of Natural Dam Lake, he noticed from a distance what he thought to be another wind-blown plastic bag caught in a mesquite.

Having checked the weather reports before leaving, he had expected a calm, cloudy morning. Then he realized that only one part of the tree was moving in the still morning air. Before he drove into the bar ditch, he knew what a branch had snagged.

To reach the pale, grayish-white creature that was hanging upside down, he parked his truck underneath the limb that held it captive. Climbing into the bed of the pickup, he realized he lacked a few inches of reaching the struggling bird.

Moving his truck backward several more feet, he climbed atop the cab. With one hand around the bird, he provided slack in the monofilament line that held it captive. Afraid of trying to unravel the plastic nightmare from the bird, he used his other hand to break the branch.

As he slid from the cab into the truck bed, he was already thinking of how to contain what he thought was a gull. Opening a large sealed box with one hand, he emptied the merchandise on the floor of the pickup. Then he proceeded to punch holes in the box with a screwdriver he had retrieved from his toolbox. Gently placing the bird and the branch inside, he closed the cardboard with duct tape.

On the way back to town, he rethought the bird's identification. Stopping by his home to let his wife see his find, he called to say he was headed our way.

"At first, I thought it was a gull," the man offered as he opened the box. Inside was a Forster's tern. As a member of the gull family, the bird could easily have been thought to be one of several seagulls migrating through our area.

Although it was the first week of September, the tern was still attired in its breeding colors. Its long, orangish-red bill was tipped in black. In contrast to the black cap that reached from its beak to cover its eyes and part of its neck, the rest of its face, neck, breast, and body were white.

Folded pale gray wings, with darker primaries underneath, led to a long, deeply forked tail that had pale-gray feathers with white tips. As we spread the wings and tail in the late morning light, the tern's silvery white feathers gave it an ethereal, almost ghostlike aura.

Soon, the black cap would be replaced with a simple black eye patch for winter plumage. The striking bold orange of its beak would disappear as it turned completely black.

Thanking the man for the rescue and delivery, we hurried to remove the fishing line from the tern. Having clipped the plastic from the branch, we started to unwind the coiling snare. How the bird had flown any distance was a mystery.

As we worked, we realized that the bird had probably acquired this mess in one of three ways. In its search for food, the Forster's tern might have hovered over an inland lake or reservoir. With its bill pointed downward, it would have looked for food floating on the surface. Plunging from overhead, it would readily dive into the water.

Another way of hunting would be to fly just above the water's surface. Without getting its feathers wet, it could have easily picked up floating insects and small, dead fish. Its other choice of dining would have been to catch dragonflies and other insects in flight.

Because of careless habits, monofilament line had been left either in or on the water, or dangling from a tree. The unsuspecting tern had been subjected to an entangling, environmental danger. Only the observant and quick-thinking driver had changed its outcome.

79. Upland Sandpiper

Bartramia longicauda

With both crop and rangeland, the woman wore two hats. When cotton had a bumper year, she was the farmer's wife. Helping her two sons load calves in their trailer, she switched to rancher's woman. Either way, her lifestyle was never dull.

Once September arrived, the woman was also guardian of the acreage allotted for dove hunters. Sometimes she wondered if the extra income was worth a broken window or holes in the sheets she had hung out to dry.

By the third week, activity had slowed somewhat. The eagerness to get their limits as quickly as possible had waned. At least now she could take her evening stroll as the sun illuminated the wispy clouds into shades of orange, pink, and purple. It was a quiet time.

As her dog rubbed against her leg, she steadied herself. His size alone had more than once knocked her to the ground. As he grew in years, he seemed to become more thoughtful of her slender, small frame.

On their way back, the animal suddenly froze. Fearing a rattlesnake, she followed his advice. Slowly inching forward, the dog approached a lump on the ground several yards ahead.

After sniffing whatever he had found, he looked back as if to summon her presence.

As she neared them both, the woman realized he had found a bird. From its coloration, she thought it might be a curlew. She knew it wasn't a killdeer. Standing over the dog's newfound trophy, she realized the bird was still alive, even though it did not rise to run or fly away.

Gently putting her hand underneath it, she planned to put the bird in her apron for the trip back to the house. Feeling moisture on her finger tips, the woman slowly turned it enough to see its belly and abdomen. From underneath the feathers came a few droplets of blood.

Having treated everything from kids to cattle, the woman hurried to stem any further bleeding. Her dog seemed excited as she rushed back to the house. His find had already been rewarded.

With its head covered to calm it, the bird lay still as she examined the wound. After separating the feathers, she could readily tell the creature had a superficial wound similar to those inflicted upon the doves during hunting season. The woman had cleaned more than her share of doves and quail for the dinner table.

After telling me about the bird and its condition, the woman was unsure of what she had. Telling her we were on our way, I grabbed several bird books before heading north of town.

At the ranch house, we eliminated her identification even though the bird had the streaked-brown wings and back that resemble a curlew's markings. We felt she had a sandpiper. Although they are similar in coloration, this bird was smaller and did not have the long, down-curved bill. To determine which sandpiper we had was our next challenge.

With a dove-like head and a short, black-tipped yellow bill, the bird had both a long neck and greenish-yellow legs. Its long, wedge-shaped tail had black bars and ended with a white band.

The shape of its body reminded me of a very plump pear. Since it was about a foot long, with a two-foot wingspan, we could verify that the woman and her dog had rescued an upland sandpiper.

Although classified as a shorebird, the sandpiper lived and hunted in pastures and prairies of the Midwest. Seldom was it seen near water. To us, it was a living "contradiction in terms."

As we talked about its characteristic way of landing, then holding its wings high above its back before folding them against its body, the woman realized she had seen the specie more than she knew. She had also seen the sandpipers running, then stopping suddenly as they hunted and snared grasshoppers and beetles. To learn that the bird also had a diet of cotton boll weevils, grubs, cutworms, and army worms, made her appreciate their natural ability to help both farmers and ranchers.

A week later, we were able to convey the good news from the wildlife center. Responding to the care and diet it had been given, the sandpiper had a chance to return to the wild. Although its migration had been halted, the "prairie dove" would someday return to ancient breeding grounds.

80. Red-tailed Hawk

Buteo jamaicensis

LATE IN THE AFTERNOON after a successful hunt, the bird soared with the sun's rays highlighting its distinguishing color. Seeing a wooden utility pole set a few feet back from the divided highway, it flapped its powerful wings.

Wanting to gain the momentum it needed to swoop quickly upward to land for a night's stay, the bird suddenly plummeted toward the ground and tumbled in the grassy median.

During her early morning drive to work the next day, a woman endured erratic

drivers as just one more challenge of maneuvering through traffic. Tomorrow would bring the same surge to hurry toward a day's pay.

Changing lanes, she passed a highway patrolman who had stopped a speeder. With another reckless driver approaching rapidly in the right lane, she remained in the left- hand lane. Ahead, she noticed a large brown object standing in the grass. As she passed, she realized it was a hawk. Glancing in the rearview mirror, she noticed that the bird did not move.

With the constant noise the raptor was enduring, she wondered why it remained in the median. Consoled by the fact that traffic would lessen after rush hour and the bird might leave, she arrived at work. Troubled by her continuing concerns about the hawk, she placed a call to Parks & Wildlife. "It may be gone by the time you get there," she added, after giving a precise location of the bird.

Often, the wildlife department in San Angelo notified volunteers that one of their game wardens had brought a bird to the office. This call was different. Repeating the instructions of the hawk's location to Diane and Dale Tracy, the receptionist did not offer any assistance in retrieving the bird. In spite of not knowing whether the raptor would still be in the median, the couple set out to find the hawk. Due to the woman's explicit instructions, it was

exactly where she said it would be.

With gloved hands, Diane neared the hawk from behind as her husband readied the carrier. Pressing the wings to the body, she realized the weight and strength of the raptor as she placed the bird in the carrier.

After telling me she did not think the red-tailed hawk could see, the volunteer listened carefully as we discussed how to handle and feed the bird. Diane and her husband are an important extension of our efforts in caring for and transporting wild birds. Recruited by Texas Parks and Wildlife in San Angelo, both are listed on our state license.

We agreed to meet in Sterling City the next day. Transferring the female raptor to our carrier, we knew this red-tailed hawk was the largest we had ever handled. Dark brown above, with creamy chest, pronounced belly-band, and rufous tail, she was the epitome of an eloquent bird of prey. Her feathers were in immaculate condition. Her body fat indicated she had dined well. She was also blind.

Since Diane and Dale wondered why Parks & Wildlife did not pick up the bird, we shared with them the same problem that exists in our area. When all the game wardens are working enforcement issues or there was a specified hunting season, there are no additional officers to send.

Once home, we watched the hawk's

reactions. Placing a hand near her face brought no response. Without vision, the bird could not see its food. In the wild, she would have starved to death. Lack of sight also explained why the bird did not move around in the median. She simply could not see where she was going.

Sounds and movement, however, were stressful to the hawk. Since her only defenses were hearing and feet, the bird struck with open talons at any perceived threat. We would have to be especially careful when removing her from the carrier.

As we prepared mice for her first feeding, I remembered another blind red-tailed hawk. Unaware of what could happen, I accidently jostled a cardboard box used for its delivery. As I reached for its legs, with my hand protected by only a leather gardening glove, I instantly learned how deep talons could penetrate.

Screaming in pain, I told Art to stop as he approached to help pry the bird's talons from my hand. Quickly telling him that with every movement, the hawk increased its grip, I asked him to get a pot from the kitchen and fill it with water. "What do you want with water?" was his natural response. "Pour it on the hawk! It'll make it let go! Hurry!" I encouraged as he disappeared into the house. Doused with water, the surprised hawk released its grasp and gave me the precious second I needed to get my hand out of the box. That was a painful but important lesson. I never let my guard down again.

For three days, we force-fed this red-tailed hawk. Prying open her bill, one hand kept it gaping while the other placed mice at the back of her throat. As the days passed, it seemed as if she were responding to movement.

Taken to one of the veterinarians serving the wildlife center in Lubbock, the hawk had suffered head trauma that resulted in the loss of sight. Turbulence created by the down-draft of a semitrailer could have slammed the raptor to the ground. Detecting vision returning in one eye, the doctor felt the other eye would recover. At least she had started noticing shadows.

For another week, the manager force-fed the red-tailed hawk. Before leaving for the weekend, she placed the bird in a small mew so that it could move around. Short-handed, the center's staff left a platter of mice for the hawk, but did not have time to force-feed it. Both the manager, upon her return, and staff were surprised to learn that the raptor could not only see her food, but was starting to eat on her own.

During the next month, the hawk became so active, she was moved to the flight cage. Some forty days after being found by the side of a road, the red-tailed hawk was taken by a volunteer to a release site. As the man opened the carrier's door, the hawk looked at him, then flew to a nearby tree. Glancing back, the raptor turned, and with renewed vigor, flew until becoming a mere speck in the distance. Soon, her eyesight, coupled with strength and agility, would lead her to rats and mice, ground squirrels, rabbits, and snakes. Her cry of kree-e-e-e-e would announce that the huntress had returned.

SCREAMING IN PAIN, I TOLD ART TO STOP AS HE APPROACHED TO HELP PRY THE BIRD'S TALONS FROM MY HAND.

81. Barn Swallows

Hirundo rustica

When I asked my friend whether her birds had left for the winter, she amazed me with her astute observation. "No. It was as if they turned on their radar. With Hurricane Ike threatening the Texas coast, they settled down and left two weeks later."

After describing their preliminary preparations for fall migration, she said their frantic pre-flights and twittering suddenly ceased. As if cancelling their travel plans, the birds had returned to their summertime behavior.

Only after the foul weather left Texas did the swift little birds begin anew their discussions and preparations. After much bickering, they were suddenly absent when she checked on them one morning. With her story in mind, I recalled another year and a late departure.

Fall was exceptional. September rains had encouraged lantana, chrysanthemums, and red oaks into outstanding colors. Calm, mild days and cool October nights were a prelude to the seasonal "trick or treat." Nearing the anticipated night, forecasters began to warn of a Canadian front headed our way.

By noon on Halloween, the fury of an early winter storm arrived. Temperatures plummeted. As the school bell announced the end of the day, rain was being driven by howling winds. Few goblins ventured out in our neighborhood that night.

When the doorbell rang, we anticipated a costumed but cold youngster. Instead, a woman with a cardboard box pleaded, "You've got to help them."

Asking her to come in out of the wind, I glanced inside. Huddled together and unresponsive were ten barn swallows. "For some reason they didn't leave," she added as a tear marked her cheek. Reassuring her that we would do everything we possibly could, I watched as she hurried back to her car.

As I prepared a nesting area and heating pad for the birds, Art entered the utility room and announced it was 29 degrees and getting colder. Looking at the delicate flyers, he asked if I thought they would survive. "I'll know in the morning," was my answer as we closed the door in order to maintain a cozy environment.

Opening the door the next morning, I heard the familiar "wit wit" of several swallows. In their makeshift home was a family from the summer nesting season. The father was the most prominent in coloration, while the mother and offspring were duller in comparison. Some of the firstborn had helped their parents in nurturing the second, and sometimes third brood.

The male, a metallic bluish-black above, sported a reddish-brown forehead and throat that was bordered by a darker-shaded breast band. His remaining breast and belly were a delicate cinnamon to pale buff. His deeply forked tail was obviously longer than that of his mate and offspring.

Having thawed small crickets for the first feeding, I had no difficulty in placing food in the youngest swallows, which gaped in their customary way of asking a parent for a meal. The parents and older siblings, however, were only convinced that I was their friend after they were taken and fed individually several times. It was a matter of holding each and opening its lower mandible to insert the bug toward the back of the throat.

The feeding schedule was as intensive as their appetites. Later in the day, I noticed two of the youngest were going into a decline. Their failure to thrive was apparent; the extreme cold took its toll.

Sustaining the remaining eight became a challenge and would last until we had a forecast that promised nearly a week of mild weather. Our typical West Texas climate promised a release date in two to three days. My hope was that I could sustain the swallows' enthusiasm and diet.

Returned to their cup-shaped mud nest, some remained inside while the parents and older siblings hunted furiously. With long, pointed wings, they flew swiftly and seemed to catch an unlimited amount of insects in the air. What we could not see, they captured immediately. The youngest were well-fed.

When the swallows had been "all atwitter" the second day they were "home," the woman felt deep inside that their departure was close. Knowing they had another chance, she could look forward to their return the following summer. When I answered the phone, the excited voice said it all. "They left this morning!"

82. LONG-EARED OWL

Asio otus

His way was the hard way. Because of his upbringing in a northeastern state, his father and grandfather had instilled in him their ways of hunting. Since his move to Texas, he had retained the essence of what he had learned. No blinds, no feeding areas to lure the unsuspecting. Alone, with only his rifle as companion, he walked the rolling hills in search of his prey.

Overnight, the November cold front, promised by the weatherman, had arrived. After a predawn breakfast, he left camp. At times he would stand beside a tree as he listened for the telltale footfall. While waiting, he had time to reflect on previous hunts and their outcome. Underfoot, the leaves dampened by morning dew lent to his quiet approach to a dense thicket.

Ever careful of what might lie ahead, he took seriously the locals' admonition regarding the feral hogs and rattlers that could be awaiting him as the day lengthened. These dangers were just a part of meeting nature on its terms.

Ahead was an old stump left by some careless soul in too big a hurry to rustle some firewood. Looking backwards when he heard what he thought was a twig breaking, he cautioned himself not to stumble over the stub if he decided to go in that direction.

Having glanced to both sides for what might have caused the sound, he froze when he looked forward again. The stump wasn't where he thought it had been. Knowing how easy it was to become disoriented in the woods, he stood still as he carefully scanned the path he planned to take. "Darn," he thought to himself, "I'd have sworn that sucker was a few feet to the left."

As his boot broke a small limb hidden by the leaves, the stump moved. Two bright yellow eyes glared at him.

In previous hunts, the man had seen great horned owls roosting in the trees. Although this bird resembled the larger owl, it was slimmer. With "horns" now fully extended, it appeared to be stretched vertically. Since it wasn't even three inches in diameter, the man had mistaken its rigid stance and rough, gray bark appearance for the remnants of a tree. The owl blinked.

As they continued to stare at each other, the owl slowly gave in to an urge to close its eyes. Since it made no attempt to fly away, the man realized the raptor was in trouble. To leave it on the ground to starve or for other wildlife to kill was unacceptable to him.

"Skinny, just plain skinny," was the description the man gave us in trying to identify the owl. His willingness to bring the bird was admirable.

Between a great horned and a screech owl in size, the slender bird of prey had suffered a damaged wing. Unable to continue its strictly nocturnal search for food, the long-eared owl was emaciated and vulnerable.

While both sexes of this specie have tawny facial discs, adult males were usually grayer and pale with more white underneath. Females, such as this one, had distinctive tawny accents on their wings, chest, and belly.

In addition to height, weight, and breadth differences in great horned and long-eared owls, the absence of a white throat was a quick way to identify a long-eared. A great horned had cross-barring on its breast, and the long-eared sported streaks running up and down.

After tube-feeding the owl, we made arrangements for delivery to the Midland wildlife sanctuary. The break in the wing had calcified. If the owl recovered from its near-starvation, it could be placed in an educational setting. Since it hunted only at dusk, early morning, or on moonlit nights, few people would ever have the opportunity to see such a secretive bird of prey. Hidden during the day, the bird had survived because it was so elusive.

As we drove home, we thought the word "long" best described the bird's attributes. Long feathery tufts, called "horns" or "ears," long body, long wings, long tail had earned its usage in partially describing the overall predator. Since this was one of three long-eared owls we would be privileged to handle, we were grateful to meet each sojourner, if only for a temporary stay.

83. Cooper's Hawk

Accipiter cooperii

Yesterday she was back. The harsh November winds had brought freezing temperatures during the night. Perched on a mesquite limb, she patiently waited for the day's meal to arrive. Her deepening coloration was indicative of the metamorphosis from juvenile to adult.

Our first acquaintance had been in a backyard in September. As the new owner of a home located several blocks away in our neighborhood, a friend called to say there was a hawk that wouldn't fly. "Can it get out of the yard?" was my first question. "No way," was her reply as she hurried to work.

Not leaving anything to chance, we hurried through breakfast and drove the short distance. Having admired her home for years because of the established trees, we had not anticipated the landscaping once we closed the side gate. An enclosed back porch looked out on a narrow patch of lawn. From there, the descent to a lower level was steep and terraced. Before walking down the stone pathway, we felt as if we were in an outdoor birdhouse. At the same height as the tops of the trees, we could readily see into the canopy as if perched on a limb ourselves. The view was overwhelming.

After searching the upper level and peering into every shrub and bush, we started slowly down the steps that had carefully been placed at the bottom of each tier. A previous owner had planted shade-loving ground covers and even more foliage to inspect. At the bottom level were several plants in which a bird might be hiding.

Concerned that perhaps the hawk had slowly inched its way upward through a large bush, one step at a time, we realized if it had gone far enough, it might have jumped to the fence top. Knowing it could then enter either a neighbor's yard or step on one of the numerous limbs offering an escape to the city park, we turned to the south to examine the last area of the yard.

At first, we saw nothing. The shade of the overhanging limbs and filtered sunlight were deceptive. Just as we were feeling defeated and ready to end our search, Art detected a movement in the shadows. Pressed against the fence was a Cooper's hawk.

With a pole net, Art attempted to catch the raptor. As quick on foot as it is in capturing prey, the Cooper's avoided the net and turned toward me.

"Don't let it get past you!" advised Art, because he could see an opportune exit for the bird. My moving in front of the bird caused it to turn just as Art quickly placed the netting over it.

Furious at being a captive, the hawk struggled against the mesh. With gloved hands, I was able to confine its wings and feet before removing it from the netting. Laying it on its back and covering its head, we examined both wings carefully. Not detecting any breaks, I wrapped the Cooper's within a towel for our ascent up the narrow steps to the lawn. Following with the pole net, Art had made a save of the day.

Calling our friend to assure her we had the hawk, I complimented her on the beauty of her backyard. "My grandchildren love it!" she said as she gave a short history of the home's background. Since the bird might have a soft-tissue injury to a wing, it would be taken to the Lubbock wildlife center for X-rays and evaluation. Whether a bruised wing or hairline fracture had caused the hawk to be grounded would be determined.

After placing the Cooper's inside a carrier, we were delayed in transporting it for seven days because of

commitments and the weather. Even though its typical attitude of contempt for anything human made it hard to handle while cleaning its quarters, the hawk enjoyed dining on small birds that constitute three-fourths of its diet. Supplied with small baby chicks provided by the center, the bird grew in strength and was one of our ornerier guests.

Readied for the trip north, the Cooper's once again resisted our handling. Taking one last look at its plumage, we noticed that the replace-ment of all but two of its tail feathers was progressing. The black bars and white-tipped ending would be with the bird as it matured.

From the brown of youth, the bird's back, wings, tail, and the top part of its head were becoming the typical mousy-gray. The thin streaks of brown on its chest that had indicated its first year were being transformed into tawny barring to accent its creamy chest and belly. Weight and wingspan indicated the hawk was female.

The next day the manager of the center related that no breaks or bruises could be found. Angry and combative, the Cooper's was placed in a mew and immediately began flying. If nothing else, its enforced incarceration had been successful.

A week later, we brought the hawk back to our neighborhood. There was no sense in giving it freedom in Lub-bock, only to have it migrate another 100 miles to where it had chosen to be. Also, it would be useful in dispersing the numerous whitewing doves and thinning their population, as they tried to dominate our winter feeding area.

Released in our side yard the mid-dle of October, the Cooper's flapped its wings and headed for the junipers along the north fence. As she landed, a deafening flutter arose from the doves as they hastily left for a safer roosting site. Seeing their departure, Art commented, "That Cooper's now knows where food is."

Soon, one morning our aggressive lady was standing on the fence outside our kitchen window. Hunting the neighborhood, she dropped by weekly as she shared her services to the sur-rounding homes. Early morning and late evening feeders, such as cardinals and thrashers, ignored her presence. Hungry, migrating seed eaters once again had a way station in their long flight south, since sparrows and doves were more cautious in their appear-ance. Nature's balance had returned.

84. *Swainson's Hawk – "Toenails"*

Buteo swainsoni

In late October, the veterinary clinic in Andrews called regarding a befuddled Swainson's hawk. "It appears to be dazed" was their description of its unusual behavior. After bringing it home, we realized what they meant.

Refusing to eat, the raptor required force-feeding. On the fourth morning, it decided to eat on its own. Then it regressed. Although the hawk seemed to improve over a week, we felt it required a trip to the wildlife center in Lubbock.

While there, we cautioned the volunteers that this bird's eating disorder seemed to indicate a serious problem with its brain telling it to eat. Otherwise, the hawk was fairly typical

Once the bird had been examined and placed in a carrier for a trip to the vet, Gail Barnes, volunteer, mentioned that we needed to see "Toenails." Describing how beautiful he was after experiencing a complete molt, she added that Tom, another volunteer, had done a wonderful job working with and teaching the hawk to be an educational bird.

"You saw the 'before,' now you need to see the 'after.'" Since this raptor was another Swainson's hawk we

had brought to the center in August 2007, we decided our next trip would include Toenails.

A few days before Thanksgiving, we made a special trip and were reacquainted with the hawk that had touched our souls. As we entered a mew on Ambassadors Row, Toenails glanced our way and began his endless chatter. Handsome, with every greasy, broken feather replaced, Toenails was the essence of the majesty of creation.

Handing me a leather glove, Gail took the ends of his jesses. As I moved my hand next to the hawk's legs, it readily stepped onto the glove. Then the leather straps around his legs were secured within my grasp.

At first, Toenails seemed somewhat wary of another handler. Accustomed to Tom and other volunteers, he knew I was a stranger. Several times he tried to fly off my hand, but the jesses limited his movement. Having to put him back on my wrist, I had no fear of his biting or footing me.

After he settled down and was content to be carried outside, Art and I slowly walked him to the pond area that was created as a soothing site where volunteers could sit, reflect, and release the pressures of rehab work. Adjoining this scenic Walden is a tiered theater for educational programs.

Continuing his verbal conversation, Toenails brought to mind that hot August morning some fifteen and a half months prior to this day. We had heard his cries from the weedy easement behind a residence as we hurried from our truck. After catching the hawk, we had discovered its feathers to be coated with a cosmetic gel or grease. Having laid the bird on its back to check body fat, I had discovered that someone had cut off all of his talons back to his toes.

Knowing that his nails might never grow back, and if they did, the talons might never be tapered and razor-sharp, I knew the hawk had been "somebody's bird." Its constant calling when approached by humans was a clear indication.

Thin, the Swainson's had escaped only to be deprived of obtaining food. With no talons, it could not roost nor pierce and hold a mouse, or even grab a grasshopper. Slowly, it would have starved to death due to the inhumane mutilation of its feet.

Notifying Gail of the plight of the hawk, I had to pause because I could not talk. Through tears, I begged for its life: "This bird needs to live as an example of the cruelty of some humans."

For the next three days, the Swainson's cried or talked incessantly. If it heard me in the kitchen making coffee, its call began. Sitting with it, talking to it, holding it in my lap, I spent those moments trying to assure the bird that its life would improve.

On the fourth day, we delivered the hawk to Gail. "It's worse than I thought," she said. Sending it to the vet, she firmly stated, "That bird will be used for education."

The drive home was less tense in knowing that the Swainson's would not be put down. Gail's phone call came shortly after we had unpacked the vehicle.

"The vet says the talons will grow back, but will never be sharp-pointed. If whomever cut them had done it when it was younger, it would have bled to death. Looks like we have another ambassador!"

As Toenails shifted his weight on my wrist, I welcomed the memories of "before and after."

Remarkable in his metamorphosis, the hawk is now the epitome of hope that rehab volunteers experience with every bird or mammal.

His constant calling also brought to mind one of the literary gems of Emily Dickinson:

"Hope is the thing with feathers that perches in the soul, and sings the song without words, and never stops, at all."

Thinking back to this experience with Toenails as the Holidays began, I'm sure Christmas came early this year.

ACKNOWLEDGEMENTS

Eos Wildlife Sanctuary, Midland, Texas
Midge & Woody Erskine, 1974-1997

South Plains Wildlife Rehabilitation Center, Lubbock, Texas 1997 -
Former manager, Debbie Tennyson,
currently "Lady Aerial," with **Medieval Times,** Atlanta, Georgia
Former manager, Gail Barnes

Wildlife volunteers

Texas Parks & Wildlife game wardens

All who brought or helped in the rescue of a bird

John A. Moseley
Managing editor, The Big Spring Herald

Bright Sky Press